EARLY EDUCATION AT HOME:

A Curriculum Guide for Parents

of Preschoolers and Kindergartners

by

M. Jean Soyke

Cover art by Sam Reilly

233 Mountain View Lane
Crossville, Tennessee 38555
(931-788-2987)

For other titles by M. Jean Soyke

Contact: M. Jean Soyke
2826 Roselawn Avenue
Baltimore, MD 21214-1719
(410) 444-1326
jsoyke@juno.com
www.athomepubs.com

Revision © March 2000
The Elijah Company
1053 Eldridge Loop
Crossville, Tennessee 38558
1-888-235-4524
www.elijahco@elijahco.com

ISBN 1-884098-15-0

TABLE OF CONTENTS

INTRODUCTION

If you are the parent of a young child today, you are truly on the proverbial horns of a dilemma. On the one hand, there is the desire to make sure your child is well-prepared for school, both academically and socially. Yet, on the other hand, there are concerns about costs, fears about health and safety, and perhaps even some guilt about sending your "baby" away so soon. For some parents, there is no choice- the home situation dictates that the child must go to school. This book, however, is addressed to another group of parents- those who feel able to keep their children at home and are wondering if they can do as good a job as the professional school. If you fall into this last category, continue reading. Yes, you CAN educate your young child at home!

UNDERSTANDING THE PRESCHOOLER: THE KEY TO SUCCESS

As American life has become increasingly more complex, we have developed an increasing dependence on the "professional". Since we find ourselves requiring the services of "professionals" for our new, complicated technology, we feel we need them in other areas as well. People don't tune their own cars any more; they take them to "car care professionals". Our houses are designed, built, painted, wired, windowed, decorated, and even cleaned by "professionals". This reverence for the "professional", however, may not be the answer when it comes to educating our children. Children are not computers, cars, or houses. They are unique human beings with specific needs that cannot always be met by someone simply because he or she is a "professional".

Does this mean that a professional educator cannot do a good job with your child? Of course not! What it **does** mean, though, is that you, as a parent, do not have to be a professional educator to meet the needs of your young child. Even in the areas where professional schools seems to have compelling advantages (such as opportunities for socialization, academic preparation, and educational materials), studies have shown repeatedly that caring, careful parents can do just as well (if not better) at preparing their children for school. Research seems to indicate that **where** preschoolers are educated is not as important as **how** they are educated.

Persons who are trained in the area of early childhood education are familiar with the term "developmentally-appropriate practice". Put simply, this means that children are presented with what they need to know when they're ready for it. This means that **anyone**, parent or professional, can provide a quality educational experience simply by being aware of the developmental needs of children and seeking to meet them. The remainder of this chapter, then, will summarize those developmental needs and offer suggestions as to how you, as the parent, can offer a quality educational experience in your home.

How Do I Know My Child Is Ready for Preschool?

Before beginning any preschool program, it's important that parents recognize when their child is ready to benefit from it. There are several indicators that show when a child is no longer a toddler, but a full-fledged "preschooler". One of the most important clues is the ability of the child to symbolize. For example, he may identify a toy car as a symbol of a real car by making driving sounds while moving it across the floor. Along with this, the parent may also notice an increase in make-believe play. The preschooler's play also becomes more purposeful, showing that he can anticipate consequences. (For example, while a toddler may try to put a square peg in a round hole again and again, a preschooler will try once, seem to think about the problem, then move to another hole.) Another indicator is a sudden increase in vocabulary (about fifty words a month), including that most-dreaded word, "why?" This shows that the child is now a true preschooler, aware of the world around him and ready to process it cognitively.

Learning Language

The number-one, all-important task for the preschooler is learning language. The primary way that this is accomplished is through interaction with more-mature speakers of the language. Participation in conversation stimulates vocabulary development, reasoning skills, comprehension, organization of ideas, verbal expression, and listening skills. Any activity your child participates in should be filled with talk. In addition, you should have plenty of opportunities to read books, tell stories, and hold discussions. Take time to listen to your preschooler and expand upon his ideas. You may feel worn out by the end of the day, but the constant chatter and questioning is all-important for your child's development.

Along with the involvement in verbal language is an increased awareness of written language. This must be handled carefully, however. Many parents are tempted to interpret the preschooler's enthusiasm and interest as readiness to begin a formal reading program. However, most preschoolers do not have the ability to hear the fine distinctions between sounds needed for phonics instruction (as seen in the child who wants to eat

4

"basghetti"); in addition, preschoolers tend to be slightly farsighted and not yet coordinated in their binocular vision (which is why books for this age group have large print). Furthermore, since several major wrist bones are still cartilage, writing is a difficult activity. (This is why young children need fat crayons and pencils and why they are taught manuscript printing before cursive, which requires more-rounded movements of the wrist.) Needless to say, workbooks and pencil-and-paper activities are not appropriate for children at this age level. Instead, parents of preschoolers should provide lots of unstructured time for their children to interact with books and point out places where print is used in our society, thus developing "print awareness".

Solving Problems

Another characteristic of the preschool age is the developing (though still limited) ability to solve problems. For the child, this is expressed in the all-important area of play. Play allows the child to learn by interacting with his environment, experimenting with the concepts he has already learned while finding out more about the world around him. In addition, play adds to his character development by encouraging him to persevere and feel competent as he successfully solves problems. Studies have also shown that children who are allowed more time to play have higher levels of creativity and use language more than those who have limited play time. The best thing that parents can do to enhance the learning that occurs in their child's play is to provide him a place for unstructured play (even if it's under a table) and to limit his toys to a few, well-chosen favorites. (Studies have found that children offered too many toys find the choices overwhelming and do not interact as effectively with them.) In addition, parents should enter into their child's play, not dominating or directing the play, but helping the child by talking with him and expanding his thinking in the play process.

Parents watching preschoolers play will notice that they have vivid imaginations. Unfortunately, these children also do not yet have the ability to discriminate between reality and fantasy. Often this is manifested at this age level in intense fears. Parents should be sensitive to their children's fears and be ready to clarify the difference between "real" and "make-believe".

Cognitive Development

Preschoolers can understand a wider variety of concepts, but they are still limited in many ways. Although they can remember events in the past and can plan for the future, the concepts of time, space, and age are still difficult for them (which is why history is not taught at this age). Memory and attention are yet fully developed, so preschoolers often have difficulty focusing on details and are easily distracted (unless they are fully interested in the activity at hand). Learning organization and classification are important tasks at this age, so parents should help by keeping "everything in its place" and encouraging their children to do the same. One of the characteristics of preschoolers that adults tend to find amusing is their literalness; for example, when they hear that someone "lost his head", they'll want to know where it was lost.

Social Development

This is an area that is often of concern to parents who educate their children at home. While it is true that preschoolers are now capable of building friendships, what is more important to them are steady, stable relationships (in other words, quality instead of quantity). They also need to be in settings where they can learn and practice acceptable social behaviors. However, it is also important to note that children of this age learn many of their social skills through imitation. Parents who educate their preschoolers at home can usually meet the social needs of their children by modeling correct behaviors and then allowing the children to practice them with selected peers in social situations.

Physical Growth

Parents of preschoolers will notice that their growth is slower but steadier, occurring mostly in the trunk and legs. This means that your preschooler has increased coordination and is ready for a wide variety of gross-motor activities– running, jumping, hopping, skipping, balancing, etc. It is important that a good part of the day be set aside for activities geared to developing the large muscles. (See the Active Play section on page 21.) One other note- handedness is usually well-established by this time, so you should know for certain whether your child is a "rightie" or a "leftie".

Understanding the development of the preschool child will help you, as a parent, in planning activities that will stimulate your child's overall growth. Although you may feel relatively confident in your ability to do this, you may still feel some hesitation. "Will I be able to provide a truly stimulating environment without all the materials the professional school has?" you may wonder (thinking about the blocks, paints, playground equipment, etc.). The next section of this book will show you exactly what is needed for a successful home school experience and how you can fit them into your family budget. There is no reason why you, the caring parent, cannot provide your child with what he needs for future success in school.

Look over the lists in the next chapter and notice how well your home school is already stocked with exciting and stimulating materials!

MATERIALS USED IN EARLY EDUCATION- AND WHERE TO GET THEM

What You Need to Buy

In preparing to educate your child at home, there are some materials that are indispensable. Usually the budget-conscious parent can look for sales beginning in mid-summer and purchase most of these supplies at that time. These materials include:

Balls (large and small)

Crayons (thick)

Pencils (thick)

Paste

Paintbrushes (various sizes)

Construction paper

Safety scissors

Drawing paper

Water color paints

What You Can Find at Home

Most of the other materials you will need can be found around the house (or collected from friends, relatives, and neighbors). The following is a list of such items that you should begin gathering, along with some ideas of how they can be used.

MAGAZINES- pictures for stories; words and letters; classifying and matching; colors; puzzles

CAN LABELS- words and letters; classifying and matching; playing store (glue labels onto large cardboard rolls); colors

EGG CARTONS- playing store; crafts; games (counting, classifying, matching, letters)

DRY CEREAL- stringing; classifying; letters (Alpha-Bits); colors (Froot Loops)

CLOTHING- matching and classifying (laundry); imaginative play; colors; practice with fasteners

BOXES- stuff and tape for blocks; playing store; doll furniture; buildings; stack and nest (sizes)

SANDPAPER- art; senses; letters

CLOTHESLINE- jump rope; letters

STRING/YARN/SHOELACES- letters; sewing cards; stringing objects

CARDBOARD TUBES- cover with labels to make "cans" for store; sizes; crafts; music

PAPER BAGS- puppets; crafts; playing store; games

JARS/PLASTIC CONTAINERS- classifying; lids for fine motor skills

BUTTONS/BEANS- counting; classifying and matching

BEANBAGS- gross motor skills

KITCHEN TOOLS- measuring; imaginative play; sizes (spoons/cups); pouring

PUDDING/YOGURT/TOOTHPASTE/HAND LOTION- fingerpainting

SCRAP FABRIC- art projects; puppets; colors and shapes; textures

RICE- pouring; measuring; colors (if dyed)

MACARONI- stringing; art projects; colors (if dyed); sorting (different kinds)

CARDBOARD- art projects; puzzles

What You Can Make

Even some of the "essentials" can be made at home. Here are some recipes for these useful educational materials.

COLORED RICE

Put a few drops of alcohol and food coloring into a Ziploc bag. Put rice into bag and shake until the color is evenly distributed. Use for pouring and measuring.

EDIBLE PLAYDOUGH

Mix 1 cup peanut butter, 1 cup corn syrup, 1½ cups powdered milk, and 1¼ cups powdered sugar together in a large bowl.

REGULAR PLAYDOUGH

In a medium saucepan, mix 1 cup flour, ½ cup salt, and 2 t. cream of tartar. In a separate container, mix 1 drop food coloring, 2 T. vegetable oil, and 1 cup water. Stir liquid into dry ingredients. Stir over medium heat several minutes until the mixture forms a ball. Let it cool in a bowl, then knead until smooth. Store in an airtight container. The playdough will keep for four to six weeks and lose its greasiness after the first or second use.

HOMEMADE FINGER PAINTS

(1) Color liquid laundry starch with poster paint. (Powdered tempera paint can also be used.)

(2) Mix 3 T. cornstarch and 3 T. cold water to make a smooth paste. Boil 1 cup water and add to paste, stirring constantly. Add a few drops of liquid detergent to make cleanup easier. Color with a small amount of tempera paint.

Fingerpaints can be used on shelf or freezer paper, on cardboard covered with white Contact paper, or on pieces of tile or plastic.

What You Can Ask For

Although it is possible to make (and scrounge) your own educational materials, some items are just nice to have. When your relatives and friends ask what they can get your child for a gift, you might want to suggest the following:

Lego/Lincoln Logs	Blocks	Wooden puzzles
Beads to string	Colored chalk	Pegs and pegboard
Housekeeping toys	Riding toys	Magnetic letters
Sand and water toys	Books	Rubber stamps and pads
Records and tapes	"Play store" toys	Musical instruments

An Additional Resource

What if you can't get-- or just don't have room for-- all of the materials mentioned here? This is where a very important resource comes in. In most parts of the country you can find support groups for people educating their children at home. Although most of these people will probably be educating older children, some will have children the same age as yours. Involvement in a home school support group can be a benefit to you in terms of positive socialization, group field trips, and sharing ideas and resources. Contact your local school board, a teaching supply store, or the supplier of this book to see if you can get help in locating a support group.

With a bit of work and a lot of imagination, the enterprising parent can find a wealth of materials for educating his or her child. Now let's get on with the "how-to's" of early education at home!

SKILLS CHECKLIST FOR KINDERGARTEN

Before anyone can plan an effective educational program, it is necessary to know what the child is expected to accomplish. The items listed below are generally accepted as skills necessary to acquire before starting formal instruction. Before beginning your educational program, you will want to assess your child to see which of these skills he or she has mastered. Also, since children of this age develop so rapidly, you will want to re-assess your child two or three times a year to keep track of continued growth. (There are spaces after each skill for you to check when it has been mastered.) The skills are listed roughly in the order in which you would expect the child to master them.

(NOTE: An asterisk indicates a skill that will be helpful for the teacher, but is not necessarily required.)

	1st attempt	2nd attempt	3rd attempt	4th attempt
GROSS MOTOR				
Climbs	___	___	___	___
Catches large ball	___	___	___	___
Bounces ball	___	___	___	___
Throws tennis ball with either hand	___	___	___	___
Walks on toes	___	___	___	___
Balances on each foot	___	___	___	___
Hops on one foot	___	___	___	___
Gallops	___	___	___	___
Walks heel to toe	___	___	___	___
Skips	___	___	___	___
Walks backward	___	___	___	___
Controlled jumping (over line, out of circle, etc.)	___	___	___	___
Swings self *	___	___	___	___

	1st attempt	2nd attempt	3rd attempt	4th attempt

FINE MOTOR

	1st attempt	2nd attempt	3rd attempt	4th attempt
Strings large beads	___	___	___	___
Uses pencil accurately	___	___	___	___
Folds paper	___	___	___	___
Puts small objects in jar or bottle	___	___	___	___
Stacks small blocks	___	___	___	___
Opens jar	___	___	___	___
Completes simple jigsaw puzzle	___	___	___	___
Traces lines	___	___	___	___
Colors within lines	___	___	___	___
Uses scissors accurately	___	___	___	___
Copies shapes and letters	___	___	___	___
Uses computer keyboard *	___	___	___	___
Zips clothing*	___	___	___	___
Buttons clothing*	___	___	___	___
Ties shoes*	___	___	___	___

SOCIAL

	1st attempt	2nd attempt	3rd attempt	4th attempt
Accepts authority	___	___	___	___
Comfortable with other children and adults	___	___	___	___
Accepts responsibility	___	___	___	___
Completes tasks	___	___	___	___
Works independently	___	___	___	___

BODY AWARENESS

	1st attempt	2nd attempt	3rd attempt	4th attempt
Able to identify different stages of growth (baby, adult, etc.)	___	___	___	___
Compares heights and weights	___	___	___	___
Knows all parts of the body	___	___	___	___
Identifies "no" areas of the body	___	___	___	___

	1st attempt	2nd attempt	3rd attempt	4th attempt

LANGUAGE

	1st attempt	2nd attempt	3rd attempt	4th attempt
Speaks in complete sentences	___	___	___	___
Tells story	___	___	___	___
Identifies letters of alphabet	___	___	___	___
Recognizes name in print	___	___	___	___
Writes name	___	___	___	___
Recognizes familiar words	___	___	___	___

COGNITIVE

	1st attempt	2nd attempt	3rd attempt	4th attempt
Identifies different textures	___	___	___	___
Recalls verses and songs from memory	___	___	___	___
Identifies colors	___	___	___	___
Classifies objects (according to color, shape, etc.)	___	___	___	___
Follows up to three directions	___	___	___	___
Identifies pictures that are the same or different	___	___	___	___
Identifies sounds that are the same or different	___	___	___	___
Tells why certain things are done	___	___	___	___
Identifies cause and effect (ex., dropping a jar causes it to break)	___	___	___	___
Gives opposites	___	___	___	___
Remembers patterns seen, then hidden	___	___	___	___
Remembers number patterns heard (up to 5 digits)	___	___	___	___
Memorizes name, age, address, and phone number	___	___	___	___
Puts pictures in sequence	___	___	___	___
Anticipates next event or pattern	___	___	___	___
Searches for answers	___	___	___	___
Reproduces drawn model	___	___	___	___
Shows increased attention span	___	___	___	___
Knows right and left *	___	___	___	___

MATHEMATICAL

	1st attempt	2nd attempt	3rd attempt	4th attempt
Identifies shapes	___	___	___	___
Counts objects	___	___	___	___
Counts to 20	___	___	___	___
Understands spatial concepts (more, nearer, bigger, etc.)	___	___	___	___

Now that you have identified your child's abilities, you are ready to develop a program that is tailor-made for your child. The first thing you need to decide is how much time you are able to devote to this enterprise. The next section will give you some guidelines for developing a schedule that will be the most beneficial to you, your child, and your family.

SUGGESTED HOME SCHOOL SCHEDULES

Professional schools meet for either full-day or half-day sessions. It is recommended that the parent use the half-day format outlined on the next page as a GENERAL guide, varying the times and activities according to the needs of your child and family. (For example, if your child is a late riser, you may want to begin later in the day and eliminate the snack time.) You may also choose to school only a few days a week, rather than every day. If you choose this option, however, do not feel that you must offer your child a full day of "school". It is far better to have only one or two half-days of carefully-chosen, fun-filled activities than for both child and parent to feel pressured by a longer program. However you adapt the schedule to fit your individual situation, a general rule of thumb is to alternate quiet activities with busier ones.

As you plan your schedule, you should also allot some time for a weekly trip. This can be a simple nature walk or a trip to the playground or library, but it is important that your child expand his or her world by venturing out into the community. The curriculum section of this book will give you some ideas for planning simple trips.

It should be noted here that some parents using this curriculum will also be educating older children at home. For these parents, the idea of "scheduling" their younger child's instruction might seem impossible. An alternate plan for these parents (one which was used by this author) is to work with the younger one separately from the older children and concentrate primarily on learning activities. (This can be done while the older children are working independently, completing household chores, or finishing their schoolwork for the day.) The active play can be incorporated with the older children's "physical education" period, and quiet play activities could be planned while the older children are completing their studies. Again, flexibility is the key here, remembering that young children will need full parental attention with most learning activities. However, many of the concepts presented can also be reinforced at "odd moments" of the day-- driving in the car, bath time, etc.

HOME SCHOOL SCHEDULE

Breakfast, dress, cleanup, etc.

QUIET PLAY (until parent is ready to begin schooling)

OPENING: 10-20 minutes

STORY: 10-20 minutes

SNACK: 15-20 minutes

LEARNING ACTIVITY (Language): 20-30 minutes

ACTIVE PLAY: 20-35 minutes

LEARNING ACTIVITIES (Math/Science/Social Studies/Health): 20-35 minutes

Lunch

Afternoon activities: nap or rest, some quiet play, and some active play (preferably outdoors.)

Let's look at each time block in depth to see what activities might be included.

Quiet Play

This is the time for self-selected, fine-motor activities that the child completes voluntarily and independently (especially good when you are busy with other responsibilities). Ideally, a certain area of your home could be set up with labelled boxes or baskets containing the materials for each activity. You can then teach your child to select an activity, complete it, then put it away, thereby encouraging independence and responsibility.

Some good activities for this time would be:

Stringing beads, macaroni, or cereal

Jigsaw puzzles

Imaginative play (dress-ups, store, etc.)

Blocks

Coloring (preferably free-hand, NOT coloring books)

Activity books (tracing, dot-to-dot, copying, etc.)

Cutting paper (Child cuts along lines drawn on paper or cuts things from magazines.)

Pegs and pegboard

Chalkboard

Egg carton games and learning centers (See Appendix A.)

Looking at books

Lacing cards

Other activities to consider (but which may require supervision) are:

Pouring and measuring birdseed or colored rice (kept in a dishpan for convenience)

Painting

Collages (gluing miscellaneous objects on paper)

Simple origami

Salt "drawing" (Empty a box of salt into a large, flat box; child then "draws"
    letters, shapes, etc., with his or her finger.)

Playdough

Stamps and stamp pad

Opening

Opening your day in a routine manner provides security for your child, helps him or her make the mental transition from "home" to "school", and sets the stage for future involvement in formal schooling. Parents can develop an opening, using one or more of the following activities.

Pledge of allegiance to the flag

Thought for the day

Memory verse

Patriotic or inspirational song

Identifying the date on a large calendar

Discussion of the weather and events of the day

Singing the alphabet while pointing to letters

Another possible opening activity could be discussing a desirable character quality. (The curriculum section of this book lists one per week.) Positive character traits are generally learned more through imitation than from direct teaching, but making the child aware of them is a good beginning. You can start by defining the character quality so that your child can understand it (perhaps by using a related Bible verse); then you can help the child identify that trait in the lives of others. You may even invent situations for discussion or role-playing to help your child understand the application of the character trait. As you go through the events of your daily lives, watch for opportunities to point out (and to practice) the character quality you are emphasizing that week. (You may even want to make a simple chart, checking off times when the trait was observed or practiced.) When your child demonstrates a positive character quality, be sure to point this out with the appropriate term. ("Oh, Billy, you were so diligent when you cleaned up those toys!") Activities such as these will give you an invaluable opportunity to discuss and to pass on the values that are important to your family.

Story

Suggestions for stories are also given in the curriculum section of this book. Some parents may prefer to use this time for Bible stories, perhaps integrating the character quality for the week. Whatever stories are chosen, they should be in easy-to-handle books with lots of colorful pictures.

Young children develop their memories through repetition; therefore, it is suggested that only one story be emphasized each week. If your child prefers, the story can simply be read over again, or you may wish to present it differently- have the child retell it for you, make puppets, act out the story, etc. By the end of the week, you should be able to ask questions about the story, and your child should be able to remember major details.

Snack

The inclusion of the snack time is completely up to you, but young children tend to eat smaller meals and often need a small snack or two to keep them going. Instead of simply going to the kitchen for something to eat, your child can be involved with you in a fun and educational experience.

Several general principles should be kept in mind here. First of all, as much as possible, the child should be involved in the preparation, creation, and clean-up of the snack; in other words, let your child do as much by himself as he feels comfortable doing. Let your child measure the ingredients; he is learning important mathematical concepts. Let him spread the peanut butter; he is developing his fine-motor skills. Let him decorate the cookies; he is expressing his creativity. Let him put the containers away; he is learning independence and responsibility.

With a little bit of ingenuity, you can tie in other educational concepts. For example, when you are teaching the color "green", make green Jello. When you are teaching the square, spread peanut butter on square crackers. When you are teaching the letter "U", make some soft pretzels in a "U" shape. There are more specific ideas in the curriculum section of this book, but the possibilities are endless!

Perhaps the most valuable aspect of the snack time, however, is the interaction that occurs between you and your child. **TALK** about what you are doing and experiencing. How does that dough feel? What's inside that egg? What will happen when we put these in the oven? How does that smell? Besides developing your child's language skills, these discussions can open the door for further learning and also solidify the relationship you have with your child. Isn't that worth a few spills and a bit of smeared jelly?

Learning Activities

Specific instructions for learning activities are given in the curriculum section, but generally these are educational experiences that **you** plan and direct.

Active Play

If possible, active play should take place outdoors. The child should be permitted to play freely, but the parent should suggest specific gross- motor activities that need to be developed, suggesting these when the child seems to be receptive. (See the Skills Checklist in the previous chapter.) If it is not possible to play outside, many gross-motor activities can be adapted to an indoor setting. You can use equipment (such as cup stilts, small trampoline, hoops for jumping, steps, jump ropes, bean bags or rings to toss, etc.), or you can always dance, exercise, or march. Give those developing muscles a workout!

You now have the ingredients you need to begin educating your child at home– but how can you put it all together? The final chapter of this book gives you an outline– the curriculum– to make sure you achieve your objectives with a program that is tailor-made for your child.

CURRICULUM

There are certain concepts that are basic to every early childhood curriculum-- letters, colors, numbers, and shapes. These may seem simple enough to teach, but in actuality there are many intermediate steps involved that depend highly on the age and maturity level of the child. (For example, it is one thing for a child to be able to trace a letter with his finger, but quite another to be able to tell what sound that letter makes.) Therefore, a core curriculum has been developed in which lists of activities are given for each concept. The activities are arranged roughly in order of difficulty, from the most basic to the more advanced. (Some of the latter are actually first-grade level skills, making this curriculum adaptable for children who are capable of working at those levels.)

To use the core curriculum most effectively, you should:

1) Look at the weekly planning guide (pages 38 - 110) and see what particular letter, number, color, and/or shape is being emphasized for the week.

2) Consult the list of activities below and choose those that are the most appropriate for your child's individual level of development, learning style, and interest. (If you are in doubt as to which would be the most appropriate, begin with the first activities listed and move up if they prove to be too simple.)

3) Write these activities in on the weekly planning sheet.

As the child successfully completes core curriculum activities, the parent can then **CAREFULLY** move on to more difficult ones. The word "carefully" cannot be stressed enough. One of the most damaging things a parent can do is to force a young child into an activity in which there is no interest, or in which the child experiences frustration or failure. If this occurs, **BACK OFF AND WAIT!** Many times changes in development will enable a child to do in January what he could not do in September. Your child does not have a race to win, and neither you nor he are "failures" if a particular skill is not mastered immediately. It is far more important that what you do with your child be **positive** and **pleasurable**, thus promoting a positive attitude toward learning.

You will notice that some activities listed have an asterisk after them. This means that the materials involved can be covered with clear Contact paper to make them permanent. (Older brothers and sisters can help with this.) Then your child can repeat the activities, using erasable markers or crayons, during times of Quiet Play-- **and** they can also be saved for younger siblings!

****

LETTERS

NOTE: At the beginning, use only capital letters. Add lower case letters only after all capital letters can be identified. (See Activity 25.)

1. SANDPAPER LETTERS. Make the letter out of sandpaper or other highly-textured material. Have your child trace the letter with an index finger, saying its name at the same time. (<u>Variation</u>: Have your child guess the letter by tracing it with his eyes closed.)

2. BODY LETTERS. Ask the child to make the letter with his body or fingers while saying its name.

3. LETTER STICKER. Print the letter being studied on a sticker and attach it to your child's clothing. Throughout the day, ask your child what letter is on the sticker. See if he can tell you without looking. (You may find it fun to give a small reward- penny, raisin, sticker, etc.- for each correct identification.)

4. CUT OUT LETTERS. Have your child find and cut the letter from old magazines or newspapers, then glue them to a piece of paper. Note the similarities and differences in sizes and type faces.

5. FOOD LETTERS. Have your child find the letter in alphabet cereal or macaroni.

6. LETTERS IN PRINT. As you are traveling, ask your child to find the letter on signs and billboards. Ask him to find the letter on merchandise in the store.

7. PLAYDOUGH LETTERS. Have your child make the letter out of playdough or pipe cleaners.

8. STRING LETTERS. Have your child make the letter with string, clothesline, shoelaces, or yarn. (Letters made with string or yarn can be glued to cardboard. They then can be traced

24

with the finger, as in activity #1, or they can be covered with paint and used as a printing block. Just make sure the letter reads the same backwards and forwards!)

9. SAND LETTERS. Let your child use fingers or stick to write the letter in sand, salt, or fingerpaint. (Note: salt can be poured into an empty gift box or cake pan.)

10. WATER LETTERS. In warm weather, let your child use a squirt bottle (or large paint brush and bucket of water). Write the letters on the sidewalk with water. (In the winter, your child can use a stick to write letters in the snow.)

11. TRACE THE LETTER. Write the letter on a piece of paper-- large at first, then gradually becoming smaller. Have the child trace the letter with a thick pencil.   *

12. BROKEN LETTERS. Write the letter on a piece of paper, using broken lines instead of solid ones. Have your child use a pencil to trace over the letter in solid lines.   *

13. COPY THE LETTER. Write the letter on a piece of paper. Have the child copy the letter next to it, or on another piece of paper.   *

14. WRITE THE LETTER. Encourage your child to fill a whole page with letters. For fun, make letters of different sizes and/or colors. For variety, use colored paper, a "Magic Slate", or a chalkboard. Practice, practice, practice!

After your child can successfully identify several letters--

15. GUESS THE LETTER. Close your eyes. Have your child use a finger or unsharpened pencil to write a letter in your hand. Can you guess what letter it is? Now switch places!

16. SORTING LETTERS. Ask your child to sort and identify all the known letters in alphabet cereal, alphabet macaroni, or letters cut from magazines.

17. MAGNETIC LETTERS. Make or purchase letters with magnetic backs. Put them in a paper bag and let your child select one. Ask the child to either identify it by touch alone or by looking at it. If it is identified correctly, he may stick it to the refrigerator or magnetic board.

18. LETTER BINGO. Good to do as an entire family! Make cards in which each square contains a different letter of the alphabet. Use markers to cover the letter that the caller names. (Rotate the responsibility of being caller among the different members of the family.)

19. LETTER MEMORY. Show a card with a letter printed on it for a few seconds, then hide the card. Can your child remember what letter was shown? (For added difficulty, show two or three cards at a time and ask the child to recall the letters in order.)

20. NAME THAT LETTER. Use the cards from activity 19. Turn them all face down. Let your child choose one and see if he or she can name it.

21. LETTER TOSS. Draw letters on the sidewalk with chalk (or on an old shower curtain with permanent marker). Let your child toss a beanbag or hop to a letter. Ask him to identify the letter.

22. LETTER SCRATCH. Write the letters of the alphabet on a piece of paper, all mixed up. Ask your child to find the letters in order and scratch out each one as it is found.   *

23. TYPE THE LETTER. Name a letter and have your child find and type it on a typewriter or word processor.

24. EGG CARTON LETTERS. Write a different letter in each cup of an egg carton. Let your child pitch a button into the carton. Ask him to identify the letter in the same cup as the button.

Match capital and lower case letters.

25. CUT AND MATCH. Let your child cut and match letters from magazines or newspapers.

26. UPPER/LOWER CASE BINGO. Play as in activity 15. This time, make cards with lower-case letters.

27. LETTER MATCHING. Make worksheets where the child must draw a line from capital letter to lower-case equivalent.   *

28. WRITE THE MATCH. Write all of the letters of the alphabet on a piece of paper. Have your child write the lower-case equivalent next to each one. (For greater difficulty, mix up the order of the letters.)   *

29. FIND THE WORDS. Find words in a magazine that have both the capital and the lower-case letter in the same word.

30. FIND THE MATCH. Place cards with lower-case letters around the house. The child is given cards with capital letters and tries to find the matches.

31. UPPER/LOWER CASE CONCENTRATION. Use the letter cards from no. 30 to play "Concentration". Mix the cards and place them face down on the table. Take turns, turning cards over two at a time until a match is found.

32. UPPER/LOWER CASE OLD MAID. Make an "Old Maid" card and add it to the cards from no. 30. Mix the cards and divide them, face down, between two players. Players find all of the matches in their hands and remove them from play. The remaining cards can be held in a fan or stack so that the other player can choose one without knowing what it is. Matches continue to be made until one player is left with the "Old Maid".

Identify the sounds of the consonants and short vowels. This is actually a skill for late kindergarten or early first grade, so do not feel you <u>must</u> teach these to your child. However, if he or she can easily complete all of the previous activities with ease and is expressing an interest in reading words, by all means, go on with the following activities.

33. NAME THAT SOUND. Place letter cards (preferably lower case) face down on a table. Ask your child to select a card and identify the sound of the letter shown. (Teach just a few letters at a time, then add letters gradually as your child masters them.)

34. SOUNDS TOSS. Play as in no. 21, but ask your child to say the sound of the letter, instead of simply identifying it.

35. MAGNETIC LETTER SOUNDS. Use the magnetic letters from no. 17, but have your child identify the sound of the letters.

36. EGG CARTON SOUNDS. Use the egg carton from no. 24, but instead ask the child to tell you the sound of the letter written in the cup.

37. TYPE THE SOUND. Tell your child a particular letter sound and have your child type that letter on the typewriter or computer keyboard.

38. MATCHING SOUNDS. Make worksheets where the child must match a picture with its initial sound. (For example, the child would draw a line to connect a picture of a dog with the letter "d".)

39. FIND THE SOUND. Give your child cards with letters and ask him to place them on objects around the house that begin with that sound.

40. CUT OUT SOUNDS. Have your child cut pictures from a magazine and glue them to a sheet of paper. He may then write the letter of the initial sound under the picture or cut the letter out and glue it under the picture.

41. SOUNDS BINGO. Make Bingo cards with different lower-case letters printed in the squares. The caller makes a letter sound, and the players must cover the letter that makes that sound. (VARIATION: The caller says a word that begins with that letter sound; for example, for the word "boy", the players would cover the letter "b".)

42. SOUNDS CONCENTRATION. Match picture cards with letter cards representing the initial sounds. Play as in no. 31.

43. SOUNDS OLD MAID. Add an "Old Maid" card to the cards from the previous game and play as in no. 32.

44. SORT THE SOUNDS. Have the children sort pictures into groups according to the initial letter sound. (For example, "dog", "door", and "dirt" would all go together.) For a long-term project, use a file box with alphabetical dividers and ask the child to place the pictures in the correct sections.)

45. PAINT THE SOUND. Ask your child to paint or draw pictures of the objects beginning with a particular sound. Write the letter of the sound under each picture.

46. LETTER BOOK. On each page of the book, write or glue one letter of the alphabet. Fill the page with cut or drawn pictures of objects that start with the sound of that letter. (For example, on the "m" page, you might have pictures of the moon, a monkey, Mommy, etc.)

If your child has mastered these letter sounds, you may want to begin a regular reading program. (See Appendix D.)

Appendix A gives additional ideas for learning centers that teach the various letter concepts.

****

NUMBERS

Before actually learning to identify the individual numerals, your child should first have a basic understanding of the CONCEPT of number- that is, "how many" objects are represented by a particular number. The first activities on this list are designed to present these initial concepts.

1. ROTE COUNTING. Count objects around the house (spoons, beans, chairs, etc.). This helps the child become familiar with the names for numbers.

2. NUMBER PICTURES. Cut pictures of a particular number of objects. For example, if you are emphasizing "two", cut out pictures of two people, two cats, two flowers, etc.

3. EGG CARTON NUMBERS. Put objects into the sections of an egg carton by specific numbers groups (ex., raisins in groups of two, buttons in groups of four, etc.)

4. GROSS-MOTOR NUMBERS. Practice numbers with your gross-motor activities. For example, when you are concentrating on the number five, you can jump five times, bounce the ball five times, etc.

5. NUMBER GROUP MATCHING. Match different arrangements of the same number. (Dominoes are good for this.) For example, put four raisins in a straight line and four raisins in a circle. Practice until your child understands that this is the same number.

After your child understands several numbers--

6. GUESS HOW MANY. Place two or more objects in a bag (or hide them in your hand). The child either feels in the bag or just guesses how many there are. Let your child count to see if the guess was correct.

7. WHO'S THERE? Knock a particular number of times. The child must guess "who's there" ("Mr. Four", "Miss Nine", etc.)

Matching objects and numerals--

8. CUT AND MATCH. Have your child cut pictures of groups, as in #2. Either write the corresponding numeral under each picture, or cut out the corresponding numeral and paste it under each picture.

9. NUMBER BINGO *(for several players).* Make bingo cards on which each square contains a different number of objects (dots, stars, etc.). Use markers to cover the picture group corresponding to the number the caller names. Rotate the responsibility of being caller among the different players.

10. NUMBER MATCHING. Make worksheets where the child must draw a line from a picture group to a corresponding numeral. *

11. DRAW THE NUMBER. Write the numerals on a piece of paper. Ask your child to draw the correct number of dots, stars, etc., next to each one. *

12. NUMBER CONCENTRATION. Make matching pairs of cards, with a picture group on one card and the corresponding numeral on the other. Play the game as in "Letters" activity no. 31.

13. NUMBER OLD MAID. Make an "Old Maid" card to add to the cards from the previous game. Play as in "Letters" activity no. 32.

14. NUMBER BOOK. On each page of the book, write or glue one numeral. Fill the page with cut or drawn picture groups representing that particular number. (For example, on the "3" page, your child might have three monkeys, three pieces of fruit, three stickers, etc.)

Identifying and writing the numerals--

15. SANDPAPER NUMBERS. Make the numeral out of sandpaper or other highly-textured material. Have your child trace the numeral with an index finger, saying its name at the same time.

16. BODY NUMERALS. Ask the child to make the numeral with body or fingers while saying its name.

17. NUMERAL STICKER. Write the numeral being studied on a sticker and attach it to your child's clothing. Throughout the day, ask your child what number is on the sticker. See if he or she can tell you without looking!

18. CUT OUT NUMERALS. Have your child find and cut out the numeral from magazines or newspapers, then glue them on a piece of paper. Discuss the differences in size and type styles.

19. FIND PRINTED NUMERALS. As you are driving, ask your child to find the numeral on signs and billboards. Ask him or her to find the numeral on merchandise in a store.

20. PLAYDOUGH NUMERALS. Have your child make the numeral with Playdough or pipecleaners.

21. STRING NUMERALS. Have your child make the numeral with string or clothesline. (SYMMETRICAL numerals made with string can be glued to cardboard. The cardboard-based letter can be covered with paint and used as a printing block.)

22. SAND NUMERALS. Let your child use stick or fingers to write the numeral in sand, salt, or fingerpaint. (In the winter, your child can also write in the snow.)

23. WATER NUMERALS. In warm weather, let your child use a squirt bottle (or large paint brush in a bucket of water) to write the numeral on the sidewalk.

24. TRACE THE NUMERAL. Write the numeral on a piece of paper-- large at first, then increasingly smaller. Have the child trace the numeral with a thick pencil. *

25. BROKEN NUMERALS. Write the numeral on a piece of paper, using broken lines instead of solid ones. Have your child use a pencil to trace over the letter in solid lines. *

26. COPY THE NUMERAL. Write the numeral on a piece of paper. Have your child copy the numeral next to it, or on another piece of paper. *

27. WRITE THE NUMERAL. Give lots of opportunity for your child to write the numeral-- in different sizes, different colors, different media, etc. Use a "Magic Slate" for more practice.

After your child can identify several numerals--

28. GUESS THE NUMERAL. Close your eyes. Have your child use a finger to draw a numeral in your hand. Can you guess which one it is? Change places.

29. SORTING NUMERALS. Ask your child to sort numerals cut from magazines or newspapers.

30. MAGNETIC NUMERALS. Make or purchase numbers with magnetic backs. Put them in a paper bag and let your child select one. Ask your child to identify it by touch alone or by looking at it. If it is identified correctly, it can be placed on the refrigerator or magnetic board.

31. NUMERAL BINGO *(for several players).* Make bingo cards on which each square contains a different numeral. Use markers to cover the numeral that the caller names. (Rotate the responsibility of being caller among the players.)

32. NUMERAL MEMORY. Show a card with a numeral printed on it for a second or two, then hide the card. Can your child remember what numeral was shown?

33. NAME THAT NUMERAL. Use the cards from the previous game. Turn them all face down. Let your child choose one and see if he or she can name the numeral.

34. NUMERAL TOSS. Draw numerals on the sidewalk with chalk. Let your child toss a beanbag or hop on a numeral. Ask your child to identify that numeral.

35. NUMERAL SCRATCH. Write the numerals on a piece of paper, all mixed up. Ask the child to find each numeral and scratch it out.

36. TYPE THE NUMERAL. Name a numeral and have your child type it.

37. EGG CARTON NUMERALS. Write a different numeral in each cup of an egg carton. Let your child toss a button into the egg carton (or put the button in the carton, close the lid, and shake it). When the button lands in a particular cup of the carton, the child must identify that numeral.

Again, there are many more activities that can be used to teach your child numbers. (Some ideas for learning centers, for example, can be found in Appendix A.) Feel free to invent your own games and learning activities-- you are limited only by your own imagination!

****

SHAPES

1. SANDPAPER SHAPES. Make the shape out of sandpaper or other highly-textured material. Have your child trace the shape with an index finger, saying its name at the same time.

2. BODY SHAPES. Ask your child to make the shape with his body or fingers while saying its name.

3. SHAPE STICKER. Draw the shape on a sticker (or locate a sticker the same shape) and attach it to your child's clothing. Throughout the day, ask your child what shape is on the sticker. See if he can tell you without looking!

4. CUT OUT SHAPES. Have your child find and cut shapes out of magazines or newspapers and glue them to a sheet of paper.

5. FOOD SHAPES. Identify foods of a particular shape-- crackers, cereals, etc.

6. FIND SHAPES. As you are driving, or while you are in the store, ask your child to find objects of a particular shape.

7. PLAYDOUGH SHAPES. Have your child make the shape out of playdough or pipecleaners.

8. STRING SHAPES. Have your child make the shape out of string or clothesline. (Letters made from string can be glued to cardboard and used as a printing plate.)

9. SAND SHAPES. Let your child use fingers or stick to draw the shape in sand, salt, or fingerpaint. (In winter, draw the shapes in the snow.)

10. WATER SHAPES. In warm weather, let your child use a squirt bottle or large paintbrush in a bucket to draw the shape with water.

11. TRACE THE SHAPE. Draw the shape on piece of paper. Have your child trace it with thick pencil. *

12. BROKEN SHAPES. Draw the shape on a piece of paper, using broken lines instead of solid ones. Have the child trace over the shape in solid lines. *

13. COPY THE SHAPE. Draw the shape on a piece of paper. Have your child copy the shape next to it or on another piece of paper. *

14. DRAW THE SHAPE. Give ample opportunity for your child to practice drawing the shape on paper, on a "Magic Slate", or other medium.

15. SHAPE DESIGN. Have your child draw the shape in different colors and sizes to create a design.

After your child can successfully identify several shapes--

16. GUESS THE SHAPE. Close your eyes. Have your child use his finger to trace a shape in your hand. Can you guess which shape it is? Now ask your child if you can do the same!

17. SORTING SHAPES. Ask your child to sort blocks or household items into different shapes.

18. SHAPE BINGO. Make bingo cards on which each square contains a different shape. Use markers to cover the shape that the caller names. (Rotate the responsibility of being caller among the players.)

19. SHAPE COLLAGE. Have your child cut shapes from different colors of paper and glue them on another paper to create a picture or design.

20. SHAPE MOBILE. Help your child make a simple coat-hanger or embroidery hoop mobile, using cut-paper shapes of different sizes and colors.

21. OBJECT TRACING. Let your child trace around different household objects and identify the shapes they make.

22. SHAPE MEMORY. Make cards which contain pictures of different shapes. Show a card for a second or two, then hide it. Can your child identify the shape? *(For added difficulty, draw two or three shapes on a card and see if your child can remember them in order.*

23. SHAPE TOSS. Draw shapes on the sidewalk with chalk. Let your child toss a beanbag or hop on a particular shape. Ask him to identify the shape.

24. EGG CARTON SHAPES. Draw a shape in each cup of an egg carton. Let your child toss a button into the egg carton and identify the shape in the cup where the button lands.

25. SHAPE BOOK. On each page, draw or glue a different shape. The child should fill the page with cut pictures or drawings of objects of that particular shape. (For example, the "square" page could have a picture of a cracker, a stamp, etc.)

26. TANGRAM. *(See Appendix B.)* A tangram is a Chinese puzzle in which a large square is cut into various shapes. These shapes are then rearranged to create various "pictures". Glue the tangram sample from Appendix B to a sheet of heavy cardboard and cut out the different pieces. Let your child see how many pictures he can copy by rearranging the tangram pieces. Talk about the shapes of the pieces as he is working.

****

COLORS

1. COLOR NAMING. Use color words in describing household objects until your child is familiar with the color names.

2. COLOR ART. In any art activity, discuss the colors involved.

3. CUT OUT COLORS. Have your child cut out objects of a particular color from newspapers or magazines.

4. COLOR OF THE WEEK. When a particular color is emphasized, make it the "color of the week". Wear an article of clothing that color every day. Eat a food of that color every day. Let objects of that color occupy a special place for the week. Be creative!

After your child can identify several colors--

5. COLOR SORTING. Have your child sort blocks, cereal, clothing, etc., by color. (For added difficulty, make a set of shapes that vary in color and size as well. Your set could include a large red square, a large blue square, a small blue square, a small blue circle, etc. Let your child separate first by color, then by size, then by shape.)

6. COLOR GAMES. Play "Candy Land" or similar game where colors are matched. Name the colors as you play.

7. GUESS THE COLOR. Choose several small objects of different colors. Hide one in your hand. Give your child three guesses as to the color of the hidden object.

8. I SPY. Look at an object in the room, but don't tell what it is. Instead, say, "I spy something _____ ", naming the color. The child must guess what the object is-- then it's **your** turn to guess!

9. COLOR BINGO. Make bingo cards on which each square is a different color. Use markers to cover the square of the color named by the caller. Rotate the responsibility of caller among the various players.

10. COLOR MEMORY. Make cards of different colors, but with backs the same. Show a card for a second or two, then hide it. Can your child guess the color that was shown?

11. NAME THAT COLOR. Place the cards from the previous game face down. Let your child choose one and see if he can name the color.

12. COLOR TOSS. Color small areas on a sidewalk with chalk. Let your child toss a beanbag or hop on a color and identify it.

13. EGG CARTON COLORS. Color the cups of an egg carton in different colors. Let your child toss a button into the carton and identify the color on which it lands. (You can also use cups of different colors for this game.)

14. COLOR BOOK. On each page, glue or draw pictures of objects that are a particular color. (For example, the red page might contain pictures of an apple, a brick house, a rose, etc.)

After your child has mastered all of the major colors--

Once your child is familiar with the colors, you may want to work on identifying the color names in print. Some of the activities from the "Letters" section, particularly numbers 25-46, can be adapted for this purpose.) However, this is an advanced activity, so pursue it only if your child is capable and interested.

****

You can integrate these core curriculum activities into the overall plan for the year. The next section gives you ideas and materials for planning your child's complete educational program.

WEEKLY PLANNING GUIDES

On the following pages, you will find weekly planning guides for an entire school year (36 weeks). (Most people will start with Week 1 in September, so seasonal activities have been added accordingly. If you are not using the curriculum in this manner, consult the index for assistance in rearranging these activities.) In addition to the core curriculum emphases, specific topics are listed in the areas of language, math, science, social studies, health, safety, manners, and character. You will also find suggestions for activities to help develop these topics, as well as ideas for related stories, snacks, and field trips.

The first thing you will want to do is choose your core curriculum activities for the week and write them in on the spaces provided. You can then look at the other activities listed and cross out the ones that you do not plan on using that week. PLEASE DO **NOT** THINK YOU MUST COMPLETE **EVERY** ACTIVITY ON THE LIST! There are many more ideas listed than you will have time, energy, or resources to complete. Also, if you are working with a younger child (3 or 4), you can reserve more difficult activities for the following year. You only need to choose a FEW to fit into your individual schedule. In addition, if you have a wonderful, creative, unique idea for a particular topic, you can write it in on the extra space provided. Trim a little, add a little, and you will have a curriculum plan tailored for your particular child and family.

If you feel the need for additional organization, special planning sheets can be found in Appendix E. The Daily Planning Sheet will enable you to follow your plans more precisely, and it even allows you to list the materials you will need so that everything is prepared ahead of time. The Week-At-A-Glance Sheet allows you to spread your chosen activities over an entire week, making sure you don't do too much of any one activity on any particular day. You may make as many copies of either planning sheet as you may need.

Once you have completed your weekly planning guides, you're ready to begin the excitement, adventure, and challenge of educating your young child at home.

WEEKLY PLANNING SHEET 1

LETTER: A

_____

_____

COLOR: Red

_____

_____

LANGUAGE: Identify and print name

(NOTE: This may take some time for your child to master. Start with activity 1 and work your way up to activity 6, taking as much time as necessary. You may need to work on this for several weeks or even months.)

1. Trace with finger over name adult has printed. (Use both capital AND lower-case letters.)

2. Trace with large pencil over name adult has printed.

3. Trace over name adult has written in broken-line letters.

4. Copy name adult has written on separate sheet of paper.

5. Write name alone.

6. Let child label personal belongings.

SOCIAL STUDIES: Family members (Choose activities for this week AND next week.)

Look at family album.

Write an experience story about a family member. (<u>Experience Story</u>: The child dictates a story of two or three sentences to an adult, who prints it correctly on a piece of paper, using both capital and lower-case letters. The child then illustrates the story, and it is kept for re-reading later.)

Collect items from each member of the family and put them in a bag. Let the child draw them out, one at a time, and tell to whom the items belong.

_____

_____

STORIES: Bridwell, Norman. The Clifford books.
                 Eastman, P. D. Are You My Mother?
                 Galdone, Paul. The Little Red Hen.
                 Kraus, Robert. Whose Mouse Are You?
                 Meeks, Esther K. Families Live Together.
                 Perrault, Charles. Little Red Riding Hood.
                 Reyher, Rebecca Hourwich. My Mother is the Most Beautiful Woman in the
                     World.

BIBLE STORY: Creation
                     Adam, Aaron, or other character starting with A

CHARACTER QUALITY: Creativity

Relate this quality to the Biblical story of creation.

Plan art projects that will allow your child to express creativity.

SNACKS: Red foods (cherries, Jello, etc.)

           Homemade applesauce, for A
                 Place 3 cored, sliced apples into 2 c. water. Boil until soft. Mash, or run
                 through food processor or blender. Add sugar and cinnamon, if desired.

TRIP: Visit a relative

Visit another family and compare it to your own

WEEKLY PLANNING SHEET 2

LETTER: B

_____

_____

COLOR: Blue

_____

_____

NUMBER: 1

_____

_____

SOCIAL STUDIES: Family members

Make a simple family tree. Use snapshots, if they are available.

Cut pictures of families out of magazines. Compare and contrast.

Cut people out of magazines to make popsicle-stick puppets or a paper-doll family. (Use later for Quiet Play.)

Have your child dictate a letter to a family member. Enclose a picture drawn by your child. Mail the letter together.

_____

_____

_____

_____

STORIES: McCloskey, Robert. <u>Blueberries for Sal.</u>
                  Seuss, Dr. <u>The Butter Battle Book.</u>

_____

BIBLE STORY: Adam and Eve
             Bartemaeus, or other character starting with B

CHARACTER QUALITY: Determination

Act out situations where determination is important (such as finishing a difficult task).

SNACKS: Butter, for B
        Put ½ pint heavy whipping cream and 1 t. salt in a jar. Cap tightly and shake
        well until most of the liquid becomes solid. Pour off remaining liquid;
        squeeze the butter lightly to remove additional liquid. Spread and eat!

        Biscuits (Your child can help with canned ones.)

        Blueberries

        Bananas (or homemade banana bread)

TRIP: Duckpin bowling (for B, or to help your child practice determination)

        Miniature golf (to practice determination)

NOTE: In Week 4, your child will begin learning some basic rules concerning health, safety, and manners. To help reinforce learning, you may want to prepare for one of the following ongoing projects.

Staple some sheets of paper together to make a Good Health, Safety Rules, and/or Good Manners book. As each rule is presented, write it at the top of a new page. Let your child find and cut out a magazine picture that exemplifies that rule.

Make a chart that lists good health, safety, and/or etiquette rules. Let your child color in a square or put on a sticker every time he or she complies with a particular rule.

LETTER: C

_____

_____

COLOR: Yellow

_____

_____

NUMBER: 2

_____

_____

SCIENCE: Autumn

Let your child choose a tree and observe the changes that occur over the next few weeks. Keep a record of the changes your child notices.

Collect autumn leaves. Discuss their similarities and differences.

Let your child choose some interesting autumn leaves to place on a piece of paper. Let him spatter paint over the leaves. Lift leaves carefully to see the outlines.

Place an autumn leaf on a table so the underside is facing up. Have your child place a piece of paper over the leaf and rub with crayons. Notice the designs of the leaf veins showing through.

_____

STORIES: Freeman, Don. <u>Corduroy.</u>
            Maass, Robert. <u>When Autumn Comes.</u>
            Provensen, Alice and Martin. <u>The Seasons at Maple Hill Farm.</u>
            Sterling, Dorothy. <u>Fall is Here.</u>
            Tresselt, Alvin. <u>Autumn Harvest.</u>

_____

BIBLE STORY: Noah

                          Cornelius, Caleb, or other character starting with C

CHARACTER QUALITY: Obedience

Relate this quality to the Biblical story of Noah.

Play "Mother, May I?", "Simon Says", or "Follow the Leader".

SNACKS: Yellow foods (bananas, corn, etc.)

                      Chicken nuggets, for C

                      Carrot and/or celery sticks, for C

                      Crackers, for C

                      "C" hot dogs

Make slashes along one side of a hot dog (NOT chicken or turkey), starting about an inch from either end. The slashes should go about half-way through the hot dog and be about ¼ inch apart. As the hot dog boils, it will curl into a "C" shape.

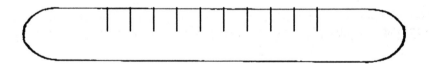

TRIP: Apple orchard

                      Farmers' market

                      Nature walk

                      Football game

LETTER: D

_____

_____

COLOR: Green

_____

_____

NUMBER: 3

_____

_____

SCIENCE: Autumn

Have your child select some autumn leaves, acorns, etc. Glue to make a collage or arrange into an interesting centerpiece for your table.

Create an autumn tree. Draw a tree trunk (or cut one from brown paper). Tear small pieces of yellow, orange, and red paper and glue them to the tree trunk. (OR dip small sponge squares into yellow, orange, and red paint and dab onto the tree trunk).

Make a "Fall Book". Cut pictures from magazines that show autumn activities. Glue to sheets of paper. Decorate a cover and staple together to make a book.

Find pictures of squirrels, bears, and migrating birds. Write an experience story for each animal (See Week 1.), telling how it gets ready for winter. (OR act out how the animals get ready for winter.)

_____

_____

SAFETY: On the street
   1. Do not cross streets alone.
   2. Obey traffic signs and lights.
   3. Do not talk to, take candy from, or ride with strangers.
   4. Do not ride toys into the street.
   5. Do not sit on the curb.
   6. Do not chase balls into the street.
   7. Cross only at corners and crosswalks. Do not cross between parked cars.

Use toy people, paper dolls, or puppets to act out street safety situations.

Make a stop light. Cover a clean, empty milk carton with dark paper. Cut out circles from red, yellow, and green construction paper. Glue the circles into place.

Watch for safety signs as you are driving.

Use tape or chalk to make an imaginary street (with sidewalks and crossings) on your sidewalk or driveway. Practice good safety habits. (VARIATION: Let your child be a policeman and "catch" you using poor safety habits.)

STORIES: Asbjornsen, Peter Christen. The Three Billy Goats Gruff.
                  Cauley, Lorinda Bryan. Goldilocks and the Three Bears.
                  Emberly, Ed. Green Says "Go".
                  Galdone, Paul. The Three Little Pigs.
                  Seuss, Dr. Green Eggs and Ham.
                  Zacharias, Thomas. But Where Is the Green Parrot?

BIBLE STORY: Abraham
                     David, Daniel, or other character beginning with D

CHARACTER QUALITY: Courage

Discuss the difference between courage and foolhardiness (in relation to safety rules).

Act out situations where courage is required (ex., another child asks him or her to do wrong).

SNACKS: Green foods (peppers, cucumbers, grapes, etc.)

               Dates, for D

               Doll salad, for D
                     Use a peach or pear half for body and a scoop of cottage cheese for head.
                     Use celery or carrot sticks for arms and legs. Raisins or nuts can be eyes,
                     nose, and mouth, and shredded cheese or carrots can be used for hair.

TRIP: Nature walk (Practice good safety habits on the street!)

WEEKLY PLANNING SHEET 5

LETTER: E

_____

_____

COLOR: Brown

_____

_____

NUMBER: 4

_____

_____

SAFETY: On the playground
1. Do not throw rocks or sand.
2. Do not "show off" on playground equipment.
3. Wait until the slide is clear before coming down.
4. Do not walk behind swings.
5. Do not stand up on swings.

When on the playground, point out children using good playground safety habits.

Write an experience story (See Week 1.) about a child at the playground who is using good safety habits.

_____

_____

MATH: Same/different

Place different small objects in a line. Ask your child to copy the pattern with the same objects. (This can also be done with beads or cereal on a string.) For added difficulty, use a repeating pattern and ask your child to predict which object would be next.

Have your child help you sort silverware or laundry. Discuss why particular objects are the same or different.

At the grocery store, ask your child to locate items that are the same as the items pictured on coupons. (If you don't use coupons, or if this proves to be too difficult for your child, save a few small labels or box fronts that your child can use to help you locate items.)

Play "Copy Me". Make a funny face, or strike a funny pose. Your child should imitate what you do. Then change places!

Make a smear image. Fold a piece of paper in half. Have your child draw a design with a crayon or pencil on one half of the paper only, pressing heavily. Fold the paper again to smear the design on the other half of the paper.

STORIES: DeRegniers, Beatrice Schenk. <u>May I Bring a Friend?</u>
             Galdone, Paul. <u>Town Mouse, Country Mouse.</u>
             Hill, Elizabeth Starr. <u>Evan's Corner.</u>

BIBLE STORY: Joseph
                 Elijah, or Elisha, or other character starting with E

CHARACTER QUALITY: Contentment

Discuss with your child how commercials and advertisements make people discontented.

Make a list of things your child already has and encourage him to express contentment with those.

SNACKS: Brown foods (peanut butter, nuts, etc.)

            Hard-cooked eggs, for E (or make egg salad)

            Homemade pretzels
                In a large bowl, mix together 1 pkg. yeast, 1½ c. warm water, 1 T. sugar, and 1 T. salt. Stir in 4 cups of flour. Knead until smooth. Shape dough into pretzel shapes, animals, letters, numbers, etc. Brush with beaten egg and sprinkle with salt. Bake at 425º F. for 15 minutes or until browned.

TRIP: Playground or park (Use good safety habits!)

LETTER: F

_____

_____

COLOR: Purple

_____

_____

NUMBER: 5

_____

_____

SAFETY: Water safety
    1. Do not run around a pool.
    2. Do not wade or swim alone.
    3. Leave the water when you hear thunder.
    4. Wear a life jacket when you are in a boat.
    5. Do not stand up in a boat.

Draw pictures of people using good water safety habits.

Use toy people in the bathtub or sink to act out water safety situations.

Write an experience story (See Week 1.) about a child at the water who is using good safety habits.

_____

_____

MATH: Same/different

Make a design by gluing different kinds of seeds, beans, or pasta to a piece of heavy paper or cardboard. As the child is working, discuss similarities and differences.

Play "Which Is Different?" Find sets of objects (laundry, silverware, buttons, pictures, etc.) where three or four are the same, but one is different. Ask your child to tell you which is different and why.

Ask your child to cut out newspaper or magazine pictures of products used in your home. Have your child match the cut-out pictures to the actual objects.

Pour water, salt, or rice from one container into another container of a different shape. Ask your child which held more. If necessary, pour back into the original container to show your child that the amounts are actually the same. Repeat with several different containers. (VARIATION: Pour from the original container into several smaller containers.)

Use a flashlight to create shadows of different objects. How are the shadows the same as the original object? Different? Ask your child to guess the object by looking only at its shadow.

STORIES: Anglund, Joan Walsh. A Friend Is Someone Who Likes You.
                     Bishop, Claire Hutchet. The Five Chinese Brothers.
                     Leaf, Munro. The Story of Ferdinand.
                     Lionni, Leo. Frederick.

BIBLE STORY: Baby Moses
                     Felix, Festus, or other character starting with F

CHARACTER QUALITY: Decisiveness

Give your child a choice of food or clothing. Say "1, 2, 3- PICK!" to encourage the child to make a prompt decision.

SNACK: Purple foods (grapes)

                Fruit, for F

                Fruit leather, for F
                     Preheat oven to 400° F. Puree any ripe fruit. Pour into greased jelly roll pan in a thin layer. Place pan in oven and lower temperature to 180° F. Cook until dry. Peel from pan and cut with scissors into strips. (Fruit leather strips can be rolled in waxed paper and frozen.)

                Fish nuggets or sticks, for F

TRIP: Indoor pool (Practice good safety habits!)

LETTER: G

_____

_____

COLOR: Orange

_____

_____

NUMBER: 6

_____

_____

SHAPE: Square

_____

_____

SAFETY: At home
  1. Keep toys picked up and off stairs.
  2. Do not play with knives or scissors.
  3. When you bathe or wash your hands, turn the cold water on first.
  4. Do not play with electrical cords or outlets.
  5. Do not play with matches.
  6. Do not use the stove by yourself. Stand back from the stove when it is being used.
  7. Do not run in the house.
  8. Do not play with balls in the house.
  9. Wipe up spills right away.
  10. Get in and out of the bathtub carefully.
  11. Do not take medicine by yourself.
  12. Know what to do if there is a fire in your house.

Fold a piece of paper into quarters. Label each section with the name of a room in the house. Have your child draw a picture of a good safety rule for each room you have listed.

Discuss and act out escape procedures for a fire. Include the "stop, drop, and roll" procedure for clothing on fire.

Plan and practice a home fire drill.

Make simple maps to show good escape routes from each room.

Practice dialing "911". (STRESS: WE ONLY DIAL "911" FOR A REAL EMERGENCY.)

Let your child be the Household Safety Inspector and check your house for poor safety practices. (You could even make an official hat or badge!)

STORIES: Rey, H. A. Curious George stories.
            Titherington, Jeane. Pumpkin, Pumpkin.

BIBLE STORY: Parting of the Red Sea
                Gideon, or other character starting with G

CHARACTER QUALITY: Trust

Blindfold your child and lead him or her around for a while.

Get a book of optical illusions from the library (to show you can't always "trust" your own eyes).

SNACKS: Orange foods

           Square crackers

           Knox blox or bar cookies cut into squares

           Graham crackers or gingerbread, for G

           Granola, for G
                Mix 2½ c. rolled oats, 1 c. shredded coconut, ½ c. chopped almonds,
                ½ c. sesame seeds, and ½ c. unsweetened wheat germ. Combine ½ c.
                honey with ¼ c. cooking oil and stir into mixture. Spread in a pan and
                bake at 300° F. for 45 minutes. Remove from pan and let cool.

TRIP: Fire station (to learn fire safety and prevention)

         Place where pumpkins are sold

LETTER: H

_____

_____

COLOR: Black

_____

_____

NUMBER: 7

_____

_____

SHAPE: Circle

_____

_____

HEALTH: Exercise and rest

Get books or tapes of children's exercises from the library. Try some!

Cut pictures from magazines showing different kinds of exercise (or people and animals at rest). Use **them** to make a book or poster.

Plan your day together to include times of exercise and rest.

Make a chart to record times of exercise and rest. (The child could color a square or paste on a sticker for each time.)

_____

_____

STORIES: Burton, Virginia Lee. The Little House.
                 Grimm, Jakob and Wilhelm. Hansel and Gretel.
                 Zion, Gene. Harry, the Dirty Dog.

_____

BIBLE STORY: Ten Commandments
Hannah, Hezekiah, or other character beginning with H

CHARACTER QUALITY: Respect

Act out situations in which we must show respect for others or their property.

Practice respectful ways of speaking to others.

Emphasize respect for everyone.

SNACKS: Round crackers or cookies

Round biscuits

Ham, for H

Hush puppies, for H

TRIP: Exercise class

Sporting event

Ballet performance

LETTER: I

_____

_____

COLOR: White

_____

_____

NUMBER: 8

_____

_____

SHAPE: Rectangle

_____

_____

HEALTH: Cleanliness
   1. Wash your hands after playing outside, using the bathroom, or playing with pets.
   2. Wash your hands before eating or touching food.
   3. Do not put your fingers in your mouth.
   4. Use only your own comb, brush, and towel.
   5. When you get a cut, wash it, dry it, and cover it with a bandaid.

Let your child examine his or her skin under a magnifying glass. (Note the hair and pores.) Look at the skin when it is dirty and again after it has been washed.

Act out what should be done when someone gets a cut. Practice on each other or on a doll.

Keep a chart to record when your child has washed his or her hands without being reminded.

Make a family first aid kit.

_____

_____

STORIES: Grimm, Jakob and Wilhelm. <u>The Fisherman and His Wife.</u>
             Waber, Bernard. <u>Ira Sleeps Over.</u>

BIBLE STORY: Fall of Jericho
                 Isaiah, Isaac, or other character starting with I

CHARACTER QUALITY: Patience

Play a game to see how long the child can sit still.

Give examples of situations where patience is needed (cooking, waiting for Christmas or a birthday, growing plants, etc.).

SNACKS: Vanilla ice cream or yogurt

            Marshmallows

            Hard-cooked eggs

            Cream cheese

            "Igloo"
                    Cut an apple in half and remove the core. Place cut side face down on
                    a plate. Use peanut butter to stick miniature marshmallows onto the apple.

TRIP: Hospital or clinic

WEEKLY PLANNING SHEET 10

LETTER: J

_____

_____

COLOR: Gray

_____

_____

NUMBER: 9

_____

_____

SHAPE: Triangle

_____

_____

HEALTH: Choosing clothing appropriate for the weather

Have your child cut pictures of people from magazines. Sort the pictures as to which clothing would be appropriate for winter, summer, rainy weather, etc.

If your child has dolls, dress them to demonstrate what is appropriate for different kinds of weather.

Have your child draw pictures of appropriate clothing for different kinds of weather. Show different temperatures on a cardboard thermometer. Have your child hold up the correct picture for the temperature shown.

_____

_____

STORIES: De La Mare, Walter. Jack and the Beanstalk.
Sawyer, Ruth. Journey Cake, Ho!

_____

BIBLE STORY: Ruth

                             Jacob, Joshua, or other character beginning with J

CHARACTER QUALITY: Kindness

Act out situations where kindness is needed.

Plan together kind things your child can do (ex., helping an elderly neighbor).

Talk about a time when someone showed kindness to your child. How did this make the child feel about himself? About the other person?

SNACKS: Triangle-shaped crackers

             Small wedges of pizza

             Jello, for J

             Jelly bread, for J

TRIP: Visit someone to whom you can show kindness (ex., nursing home resident, neighbor, etc.)

LETTER: K

_____

_____

COLOR: Pink

_____

_____

NUMBER: 10

(This would be a good week to learn a counting rhyme, such as "Ten Little Indians", or play the game of Hopscotch.)

_____

_____

MANNERS: Table manners
    1. Come quickly when you are called.
    2. Wait until everyone is served before eating.
    3. Chew with your mouth closed.
    4. Use your utensils, not your hands.
    5. Do not talk with food in your mouth.
    6. Do not put your elbows on the table.
    7. Say "please" and "thank you".
    8. Ask to be excused when you are finished.
    9. Use your napkin to wipe your face and hands.

Practice good table manners by having a pretend meal with dolls or stuffed animals.

_____

_____

SOCIAL STUDIES: Thanksgiving

Have the child draw or cut pictures from magazines of thing for which he or she is thankful.

Have the child draw or cut pictures of common Thanksgiving foods and glue them to a paper plate.

Trace around your child's hand on a piece of paper. Add a turkey's beak and wattle to the outline of the thumb and add stick feet to the bottom of the outline. Have the child color the "turkey".

Make a pine cone turkey. Glue paper feathers to the large end of a pine cone to make a tail and a paper turkey head at the small end of the pine cone.

Make an Indian headband out of paper and/or a drum from a coffee can or oatmeal box.

Have your child draw pictures of things for which he or she is thankful. Share these at your Thanksgiving meal.

Draw a paper cornucopia on a piece of paper. Let your child cut out pictures of fruit from magazines or newspapers and glue them to the cornucopia.

STORIES: The Thanksgiving story
Devlin, Wende. Cranberry Thanksgiving.
Payne, Emmy. Katy No-Pocket.

BIBLE STORY: The boy Samuel
Korah, or other character starting with K (You could also read about any of the kings in the Bible)

CHARACTER QUALITY: Thankfulness

Have your child write a thank-you note to a special person.

SNACKS: Strawberry ice cream or yogurt

Cornbread

Kabobs, for K
On rounded toothpicks, skewer hot dog slices and thawed frozen vegetables (carrot slices, lima beans, French fries, etc.). Place on a baking sheet and cook in oven for a few minutes.

TRIPS: Visit a relative for the holiday

Museum with Indian artifacts

Turkey farm

LETTER: L

_____

_____

COLORS: Review (See pages 34-35 for ideas.)

_____

_____

MATH: Small/medium/large (sizes)

Sort pencils, cups, blocks, etc.

Play "Treasure Hunt". Show the child an object and ask him to find another object in the house that is larger (or smaller). If the object is questionable, ask the child to explain his choice.

Use your family pictures (or puppets) from Week 1. Ask your child to arrange them in order from largest to smallest (or vice versa).

Find three objects that fit the "small-medium-large" pattern. Ask your child to cover his eyes. Remove one object from the pattern. Ask your child which is missing.

Have your child put measuring cups or spoons, blocks, or boxes in size order.

_____

_____

MANNERS: Manners in a group of children (school, church, playground, etc.)
1. Take turns.
2. Listen when someone else is talking.
3. Wait until others are finished before you begin to talk.
4. Say "please", "thank you", "I'm sorry", and "you're welcome".
5. If there is a teacher, raise your hand to get attention. If what you have to say is very important, say, "Excuse me."
6. Do not push or shove.
7. Walk around people who are talking.

Play "Simon Says", but only obey the leader if he or she says, "Please".

Make a "class" of dolls or stuffed animals and practice good group manners.

Play "Please, Thank You, I'm Sorry". Tell the child a situation, then have him or her tell you which phrase is appropriate. (Example: "Your grandmother gives you a cookie." Answer: "Thank you.")

STORIES: Any color books
Andersen, Hans Christian. <u>Thumbelina.</u>
Anglund, Joan Walsh. <u>Love Is a Special Way of Feeling.</u>
Anglund, Joan Walsh. <u>What Color Is Love?</u>
Asch, Frank. <u>Skyfire.</u>
Kraus, Robert. <u>Leo, the Late Bloomer.</u>
Waber, Bernard. <u>Lovable Lyle.</u>

BIBLE STORY: David and Goliath
Lydia, Luke, or other character beginning with L

CHARACTER QUALITY: Humility

Let your child be a waiter or waitress for a family meal.

SNACKS: Foods of different colors- discuss the colors

Lemon or lime foods, for L

Lollipops, for L
Grease a cookie sheet and lay popsicle sticks on it. Mix 2 c. sugar, ½ c. water, and 1 c. light corn syrup. Boil over medium heat until a candy thermometer reads 280 degrees. Do not stir. Remove from heat and add ½ t. food coloring and 1½ t. vanilla. Pour hot liquid over sticks and let cool.

TRIP: Take a walk and collect objects of different sizes (such as sticks, rocks, etc.).

WEEKLY PLANNING SHEET 13

LETTER: M

_____

_____

SHAPE: Diamond

_____

_____

SOCIAL STUDIES: Stores

(NOTE: If you begin in September, this week will most likely coincide with the holiday shopping season. If at all possible, take your child with you as you shop during this time. Use the good manners outlined below.)

Write an experience story about a store. (See Week 1.)

Work with your child to make a "pretend" store. Let your child be the cashier. (Use a muffin tin for a cash register.) This would be a good activity for the family to work on together.

Have your child cut store logos from your local newspaper. Take them with you on your next shopping trip. Have your child match the logos with the store he sees.

On a large piece of paper, label sections with titles of different stores (grocery store, department store, drug store, etc.). Have your child cut or draw pictures of items that would be found in stores and put them in the correct section.

Find out about the different workers in a store (cashier, manager, salesperson, etc.). Draw pictures of each worker and discuss his job.

_____

_____

MANNERS: Public places
1. Do not run in stores.
2. Do not touch things in stores.
3. Sit quietly in waiting rooms or at performances.
4. Answer when someone speaks to you.
5. Say "ma'am" or "sir" when you are talking to an adult.
6. If you did not hear what was said, say, "Pardon me?"

Use toy people or dolls to act out good manners in public places.

Make the pretend store, as described on the previous page. Not only can your child act out the different jobs in a store, but he or she can also pretend to be a customer and practice good store manners.

STORIES: Bemelmans, Ludwig. Madeline.
              Burton, Virginia Lee. Mike Mulligan and His Steam Shovel.

BIBLE STORY: David and Jonathan
                  Moses, Miriam, or other character beginning with M

CHARACTER QUALITY: Loyalty

Talk about ways we show loyalty (such as defending people, keeping their secrets, etc.).

Have your child make and send a card to a friend.

SNACKS: Diamond-shaped crackers

             Mozzarella or Muenster cheese, for M

             Macaroni, for M

             Muffins, for M

             Marshmallow and rice cereal squares, for M

TRIP: Stores

              (NOTE: Many stores will allow small groups of children to tour their facilities. Carvel, Pizza Hut, McDonald's, and some grocery chains do this. Perhaps you could organize a group with some other parents, check your local stores, and arrange a visit with them.)

WEEKLY PLANNING SHEET 14

LETTER: N

_____

_____

SHAPE: Heart

_____

_____

SOCIAL STUDIES: Christmas

Draw a picture of the first Christmas.

Make Christmas decorations. (Your public library has many books to give you ideas.)

Make Christmas cookies together.

Help your child string popped corn, cranberries, small balls of crushed aluminum foil, cereal, or cut pieces of drinking straws to make tree garlands.

Make Christmas cards to send or give to family members.

Observe a lighted candle in a dark room. Discuss the movement of the flame, the dripping wax, etc.

Make a calendar to mark off the days until Christmas.

_____

_____

SAFETY, HEALTH, MANNERS: Review

If you made a book as described in Week 2, have the child go through it and explain each rule.

If you made a chart as described in Week 2, make award stickers, badges, or certificates for areas in which your child has excelled. (Perhaps he or she could be Fire Safety Expert, Household Safety Chief, Miss Manners, etc.)

_____

_____

STORIES: Christmas or Hanukkah story
            Books about Christmas in other lands
            Anglund, Joan Walsh. Christmas Is a Time of Giving.
            Wells, Rosemary. Noisy Nora.

BIBLE STORY: Mephibosheth
                Christmas story
                Noah, Naaman, or other character beginning with N

CHARACTER QUALITY: Compassion

Make a list of things your child can do to show compassion for others. If possible, choose at least one thing from the list to do this week.

SNACKS: Christmas cookies

            Nuts, for N

            Nachos, for N

            Apples, cut crosswise into slices to make "stars"

            Christmas tree veggies/fruits
                Purchase a styrofoam cone. Attach small chunks of raw fruits or
                vegetables to the tree with toothpicks..

TRIP: Visit a relative or friend and compare the celebration there with your own
                    family's.

            Window shopping

            Christmas displays

            Christmas caroling

            Christmas party

WEEKLY PLANNING SHEET 15

LETTER: O

_____

_____

SHAPE: Oval

_____

_____

SOCIAL STUDIES: Christmas

Act out the Christmas story (or make simple puppets).

Make homemade wrapping paper. (Sponge-painting, stamping, or potato printing is especially nice for this.)

Make placemats for the family. Cut red or green poster board into 12" by 18" rectangles. Let the child cut old Christmas cards and glue them onto the placemats. Cover with clear Contact paper to seal.

Help your child make his or her own Christmas gifts. (You can get many ideas from children's craft books in the public library.)

Write an experience story about Christmas at your house. (See Week 1.)

Have your child create a nativity scene with blocks.

Play a record or watch Tchaikovsky's "Nutcracker Suite".

Retell or watch Dickens' "A Christmas Carol".

_____

_____

STORIES: Hoff, Sid. _Oliver._
            Thaler, Mike. _Owly._
            Zimnik, Reiner. _Little Owl._

_____

BIBLE STORY: Elijah at Mount Carmel
                          Onesimus, Omri, or other character beginning with O

CHARACTER QUALITY: Love

Identify different ways people show love.

Have your child think of a way to express love to each family member this week.

SNACKS: Cereal in "O" shapes

              Oatmeal cookies, for O

           "O" hot dogs
                  Make slashes along one side of a hot dog (**NOT** chicken or turkey).
                  Go halfway into the hot dog, making slashes about ¼ inch apart. As the
                  hot dog boils, it will curve into an "O" shape.

TRIP: Visit someone to whom you can show love (relative, shut-in, neighbor, etc.).

This week is scheduled as a holiday break. If it coincides with the week after Christmas, use this opportunity to write thank-you notes for gifts received.

WEEKLY PLANNING SHEET 17

LETTER: P

_____

_____

SHAPES: Review *(See pages 32-34 for ideas.)*

_____

_____

SCIENCE: Five senses (sight)

Have your child look at his or her eyes in the mirror. Name the different parts. Turn out the lights, then watch what happens to the pupils of the eyes when the light comes on again.

Make shadow figures, using your hands.

Play "I Spy". (See page 35.)

Read about Braille in the encyclopedia. Try to make some words in Braille.

_____

SCIENCE: Winter

Make paper snowflakes.

Cut or draw pictures of winter activities.

Make a snowy day picture, using white crayon OR splattering white paint on dark paper.

Cut pictures of trees and plants from magazines and divide them into groups: evergreens, "resting" plants (those that lie dormant), and annuals (those that live only one season).

Cut or draw pictures of different animals to show what happens to them in the winter.

Bring snow indoors and watch it melt. Discuss the changes.

Make a winter snow scene in the lid of an old box. Use cotton for snow, a small mirror for a pond, and small branches for trees. Add plastic, playdough, or paper animals.

Catch falling snowflakes on dark paper. Examine them under a magnifying glass.

Look for animal tracks in the snow. Guess what kind of animal made the tracks.

Measure the temperature indoors and outdoors.

Make a simple bird feeder and watch for birds.

>**MILK CARTON-** Cut rectangles from both sides of a milk carton. Punch a hole in top of the carton; run a string through the hole. Tie to hang the feeder. Fill with birdseed.

>**PINE CONE-** Tie a string to a pine cone and make a loop in the string. Roll the pine cone first in peanut butter, then in birdseed. Hang the feeder.

>**DOUGHNUT-** Punch holes in the center of two plastic lids. Put a doughnut between the two lids. Run a heavy cord through the holes. Knot cord at one end and tie the other end to a tree.

STORIES: Branley, Franklyn Mansfield. Big Tracks, Little Tracks.
             Keats, Ezra Jack. The Snowy Day.
             Lenski, Lois. I Like Winter.
             Tresselt, Alvin. White Snow, Bright Snow.

BIBLE STORY: Elisha
                 Peter, Paul, or other character beginning with P

CHARACTER QUALITY: Diligence

Give your child a small task. Reward him or her if it is completed diligently.

SNACKS: Marshmallow snowmen

            Popcorn

            CLEAN snow with maple or chocolate syrup

            Homemade peanut butter, for P
                 Put 1½ T. oil and 1 c. peanuts in blender or food processor.
                 Blend until smooth.

TRIP: Nature walk

          School for the blind

WEEKLY PLANNING SHEET 18

LETTER: Q

_____

_____

MATH: Opposites

Compare "heavy" and "light" by weighing different objects, two at a time.

Play "Mary Contrary". (This is played like "Simon Says', except that the child does the **opposite** of what he is told.)

Sort pictures of animals as to whether they live **over** or **under** the ground.

_____

_____

SCIENCE: Food groups (meat)

Cut or draw pictures of different kinds of meats.

Identify sources of protein that are not meat (ex., nuts, eggs).

_____

_____

SCIENCE: Five senses (sound)

Blindfold your child. Make different sounds and ask your child to identify the sound being made. (Ideas: crinkling or tearing paper, opening a soda can, a ticking clock, etc.)

Have your child close his eyes and identify all the sounds he can hear.

Tell a favorite story and let your child add sound effects.

Get a sign language book from the library and try to learn a few signs. (You may want to put cotton in your child's ears to give him the feeling of being deaf.)

Have your child identify high and low pitches. Use a musical instrument or glasses filled with varying amounts of water.

Make a paper cup telephone. (Make sure the string is taut between the cups.)

72

Create clapping patterns and see if your child can repeat them.

Hum a song and see if your child can guess what it is.

Make a Sound Box. Cut a "window" in the side of a small box or milk carton. Stretch rubber bands of varying thicknesses around the box, going across the "window". Listen to the different sounds as the bands are plucked. See what happens to the sound when pencils are placed under the rubber bands.

STORIES: Aesop. The Tortoise and the Hare.
Book of Opposites series.
Fleisher, Robin. Quilts in the Attic.
Any Tana Hoban book (Push-Pull, Empty-Full, etc.)
Isadora, Rachel. I Hear.

BIBLE STORY: Joash
Queen Esther (for Q)

CHARACTER QUALITY: Initiative

Reward your child when he or she does a job without being told.

SNACKS: Lunch meats *(can be cut with cookie cutters)*

Hot dogs

Cracker "quilt", for Q
Spread square crackers with different toppings (peanut butter, jelly, apple butter, cream cheese, etc.). Arrange in a "quilt" pattern.

TRIP: Butcher shop, deli, or meat department of a grocery store

School for the deaf

LETTER: R

_____

_____

MATH: Opposites

Find opposites in your house (ex., **open** door, **closed** window).

Cut a design out of white paper. Glue the background piece on to a sheet of black paper so that the black shows through. Then glue the white cutouts on another sheet of black paper in the same pattern. When finished, one picture should be the exact opposite of the other.

_____

_____

SCIENCE: Food groups (grains)

Cut or draw pictures of different grain foods.

String macaroni to make a chain. (These can be colored first by shaking them in a container with a few drops of food coloring or paint.)

Create a collage, using rice, corn, pasta, and other grain foods.

_____

_____

SCIENCE: Five senses (smell)

Blindfold your child and have him identify different objects by their odors (ex., onion, perfume, lemon, pickles, etc.). Which do you like? Don't like?

Smell objects that normally don't have distinctive odors (such as coins, pencils, etc.). Describe the smells.

Make a smell collage. Place drops of glue on different areas of a piece of paper. Sprinkle different spices on the glue drops. Label the smells.

_____

_____

STORIES: Carle, Eric. Walter the Baker.
             Galdone, Paul. Gingerbread Boy.
             Zion, Gene. No Roses for Harry!

BIBLE STORY: Naaman
                 Rahab, Ruth, or other character beginning with R

CHARACTER QUALITY: Hospitality

Invite a friend over. Practice good hospitality.

SNACKS: Soft pretzels (See Week 5.)

            Muffins

            Crackers

            Cold cereal (with or without milk)

            Rice cakes (Spread with peanut butter and decorate with raisins to make a smiling
                 face.)

            Raisins, for R

TRIP: Grocery store

          Bakery

LETTER: S

_____

_____

SCIENCE: Food groups (dairy)

Cut or draw pictures of different dairy products.

Separate pictures of foods into the four food groups. (For additional challenge, include pictures of foods that do not fit into any group, such as soda.)

Classify foods found in your refrigerator.

_____

_____

SCIENCE: Five senses (touch)

Place different household objects in a paper bag. Have your child identify the objects by putting his hand in the bag and feeling them. (VARIATIONS: Have your child find a particular object in the bag by touching it OR give your child an object and have him find an identical object in the bag by feeling it.)

Blindfold your child and give him an object to hold. Have him identify the object simply by touch.

Place small household objects in envelopes. Seal the envelopes. Let your child guess what the objects are, then rub over them with a pencil to see if the guesses were correct. (VARIATION: Shine a flashlight through the envelopes to identify the objects.)

Make a texture collage. Glue on small pieces of materials that are different textures (ex., sandpaper, wood, fabric, etc.).

Let your child feel different objects with his or her feet.

_____

_____

STORIES: Brown, Marcia. Stone Soap.
            Lionni, Leo. Swimmy.
            Showers, Paul. Find Out By Touching.
            Steig, William. Sylvester and the Magic Pebble.

_____

BIBLE STORY: Daniel
                 Samson, Samuel, or other character beginning with S

CHARACTER QUALITY: Responsibility

Make a chore chart for your child.

Discuss the responsibilities of each family member and their importance to the family.

SNACKS: Salad, for S

            Butter (See Week 2.)

            Cheese wedges or string cheese

            Yogurt

            Milkshake

            Hot dogs, slashed to make "S" shapes
                Slash along one side of a hot dog (**NOT** turkey or chicken), going about
                halfway into the hot dog and spacing slashes about ¼ inch apart.
                Slash halfway down the hot dog on one side, then continue on the other
                side of the hot dog. As the hot dog boils, it will curl into an "S" shape.

TRIP: Grocery store

            Dairy farm

WEEKLY PLANNING SHEET 21

LETTER: T

_____

_____

LANGUAGE: Sequence

Draw (or find in magazines) three or four pictures that tell a story. Mix up the pictures and have your child put them in order.

Have your child tell you-- in order-- how to accomplish a particular task, such as brushing teeth. Write the steps as your child dictates them.

Choose some interesting pictures in books or magazines. Ask your child to tell what he thinks will happen next.

_____

_____

SCIENCE: Food groups (fruits and vegetables)

Cut or draw pictures of various fruits and vegetables.

Make a coat-hanger mobile of different fruits and vegetables.

Match various fruits and vegetables with products made from them (ex., apples with applesauce).

Play "What Am I?" Give clues about a particular fruit or vegetable and have your child guess which one it is.

Compare fruits and vegetables in their raw and cooked states.

Divide a piece of paper into quarters to make a poster of the four food groups. Glue or draw pictures in each section.

Classify foods found in your refrigerator or pantry.

_____

_____

SCIENCE: Five senses (taste)

Blindfold your child and give him something to taste. Have him identify the object by taste.

Separate foods (or pictures of foods) by the way they taste (sour, sweet, bitter, or salty). (For advanced children, you can show them a diagram of the different areas of the tongue that respond to the different taste sensations.)

Review all five senses. Find magazine pictures of objects and classify them as to the sense by which we first experience them (ex., sandpaper- touch, food- taste).

While discussing the mouth, discuss proper tooth care with your child.

STORIES: Lobel, Arnold. <u>A Treeful of Pigs.</u>
                 Mosel, Arlene. <u>Tikki Tikki Tembo.</u>

BIBLE STORY: Esther
                      Timothy, Thomas, or other character starting with T

CHARACTER QUALITY: Self-control

Play a game to see how long your child can sit still.

SNACKS: Vegetable sticks or "kabobs" (See Week 11.)

                 Fruit slices or salad

                 Raisins

                 Tacos or tortillas, for T

TRIP: Grocery store

WEEKLY PLANNING SHEET 22

LETTER: U

_____

_____

COLOR: Red

_____

_____

LANGUAGE: Sequence

Make a pattern, using small household objects, blocks, beads, etc. Give your child the same objects and have him or her copy the pattern. (VARIATION: Make a pattern that repeats two or three times. Ask your child to predict what will come next.)

Cut out some simple cartoons from the newspaper. Separate the frames and ask your child to put them back in order.

_____

_____

STORIES: Andersen, Hans Christian. The Ugly Duckling.
            Bridwell, Norman. Clifford, the Big Red Dog.
            Steiner, Charlotte. My Slippers Are Red.
            Yashima, Taro. Umbrella.

_____

BIBLE STORY: Birth of Jesus
                Uzziah, or other character beginning with U

_____

CHARACTER QUALITY: Orderliness

Give your child two or three commands to execute in order.

Find something in the house that could use some organization (toys, clothes, books, etc.). Let your child help label and organize the materials.

Play a matching game. Match items with the places in which they are kept (ex., tools in a shed or workroom, cutlery in a drawer, clothes in a closet, etc.).

SNACKS: Red foods

Kabobs, for sequence (See Week 11.)

Cracker "quilt", for sequence (See Week 18.)

TRIP: Children's museum (Write an experience story, telling what was seen in order.)

Factory (Note the sequence in which the item is manufactured.)

Pizza Hut or McDonald's (to see the order in which food is prepared) *(See the note from Week 13.)*

WEEKLY PLANNING SHEET 23

LETTER: V

_____

_____

COLOR: Yellow

_____

_____

SCIENCE: Outer Space

Observe the sun and moon at different locations in the sky. Discuss their movement.

Use a flashlight and globe to demonstrate day and night.

Observe the phases of the moon.

Act out appropriate motions for the sun, moon, and stars.

_____

_____

SOCIAL STUDIES: Transportation

Cut or draw pictures of different types of transportation.

Use milk cartons, boxes, or blocks to create a train or bus.

Use paper cut into geometric shapes (along with macaroni wheels or buttons) to create pictures of different kinds of transportation.

Use chairs to make an imaginary train, car, or airplane. Write a story about your "trip".

Sing "The Wheels on the Bus".

Identify different types of transportation by their sounds.

Give clues to guess the different forms of transportation.

_____

_____

STORIES: Asch, Frank. The Little Bear books, such as <u>Mooncake</u>, <u>Moongame</u>, and <u>Happy</u>
                  <u>Birthday, Moon.</u>
           Flack, Marjorie. <u>Boats on the River.</u>
           Keats, Ezra Jack. <u>Whistle for Willie.</u>
           Piper, Watty. <u>The Little Engine That Could.</u>
           Thurber, James. <u>Many Moons.</u>
           Yolen, Jane. <u>Owl Moon.</u>

BIBLE STORY: Jesus at the Temple
                 Vashti, or other character beginning with V

CHARACTER QUALITY: Teachable spirit

Let your child teach YOU something (to demonstrate a teachable spirit)!

SNACKS: Yellow foods (bananas, cheese)

           "Astronaut" food (Tang, breakfast bars, etc.)

           "Rocket"
                 Mix 1 small box of gelatin according to the directions. Pour into empty
                 juice can and put in refrigerator to set. When ready to eat, dip can in
                 hot water for a few seconds. Turn upside down on plate and add a carrot
                 for the nose cone.

TRIP: Gas station

           Bus/subway/train ride

           Planetarium

WEEKLY PLANNING SHEET 24

LETTER: W

_____

_____

COLOR: Orange

_____

_____

SCIENCE: Outer Space

Make a space picture. Use black or blue construction paper for a background. Stick-on stars can also be used.

Make a rocket, using a cardboard tube, newspaper, and aluminum foil. Stuff the top of the tube with newspaper to create the nose of the rocket, then cover the rocket with aluminum foil.

Make a large box into a rocket ship. Make an astronaut's helmet out of a paper bag. Let your child pretend he is going on a space trip. Write a story about it.

_____

_____

SOCIAL STUDIES: Transportation

Sort pictures of different types of transportation by the number of wheels each vehicle has. (VARIATION: Sort each picture as to whether it travels on land, air, or water.)

Act out the different forms of transportation. (VARIATION: Play "Charades" and try to guess the form of transportation.)

Make sailboats. Use Ivory soap or styrofoam blocks as the boat. Use a meat skewer, pencil, or stick for the mast and add a paper sail. See if your boat will float!

Sing "Row, Row, Row Your Boat".

Use scrap materials (screws, nuts, bolts, washers, etc.) to make your own means of transportation (or create a new one)!

Listen to railroad music.

Use a large cardboard carton to make a pretend boat, car, etc.

Make paper airplanes.

STORIES: Brown, Margaret Wise. Two Little Trains.
                Kessler, Ethel. Big Red Bus.
                Lenski, Lois. The Little Auto.
                Lenski, Lois. The Little Sailboat.

BIBLE STORY: Calling the Disciples
                      Study one or more of the widows mentioned in the Bible.

CHARACTER QUALITY: Enthusiasm

Think of situations in which it is difficult for your child to be enthusiastic (ex., putting toys away). Act out the situation, changing "I don't want to" to "Yes, I will".

Watch the video, "Mary Poppins" (as an example of enthusiasm).

SNACKS: Orange foods

          Waffles, for W

          Carrot salad
               Mix shredded carrot, raisins, chopped nuts, and cole slaw dressing.

        "Boats"
               Use a hard-cooked egg (or celery stick that has been filled with peanut butter or cream cheese). Skewer a slice of American cheese on a toothpick to create a sail.

TRIP: Waterfront area

       Airport

LETTER: X

_____

_____

NUMBER: 11

_____

_____

SCIENCE: Spring weather

Make a pinwheel. Cut a square from colored paper and decorate it. Fold the square along both diagonals. Trace around a penny at the exact center of the square (where the two diagonals meet). Cut along the diagonal folds to the edge of the traced circle. Bend each alternate corner into the center. Push a straight pin through the four corners and the center of the circle, then into the eraser of a pencil. Blow your pinwheel and watch it spin!

Make a bird's nest from clay or playdough, then stick in twigs or straw.

Blow-paint a spring tree. Place a bit of brown tempera paint at the lower edge of a piece of paper. Blow through a straw to spread the paint upward toward the top of the page, creating the trunk and branches of the tree. Use a small sponge to paint bright green leaves and white or pink blossoms on the tree. (VARIATION: Glue torn bits of green, pink, or white tissue paper to the tree.)

Make a spring collage, using pretty leaves and flowers.

Put scraps of yarn, fabric, trimmings, and/or paper in a mesh bag and hang the bag from a tree. As the items disappear, take a walk and look for the scraps in nearby birds' nests.

Make a paper windsock. Use a large piece of paper, 12" by 20". Cut 8 streamers of paper, each 2" by 12" (or use crepe paper strips). Glue these streamers to the bottom of the large piece of paper. Bring the short edges of the paper around to form a cylinder; glue or staple. Punch holes on opposite sides of the cylinder and tie on a long piece of string or yarn.

Make a pussy-willow. Draw the branches, then glue on Q-tips or puffed rice for the buds.

Gather pussy-willows (or other buds) and observe the changes that take place.

Gather different flowers; compare and contrast. Take the flowers apart and examine the different parts.

_____

_____

STORIES: Anglund, Joan Walsh. Spring Is a New Beginning.
Gans, Roma. It's Nesting Time.
Kuskin, Karla. The Bear Who Saw the Spring.
Seuss, Dr. Fox in Socks.
Seuss, Dr. Horton Hatches the Egg.
Spier, Peter. The Fox Went Out on a Chilly Night.

BIBLE STORY: Jesus Heals the Man Lowered Through the Roof
Xerxes (also known as Ahaseurus in the book of Esther)

CHARACTER QUALITY: Attentiveness

Play games in which attentiveness is required, such as "Simon Says" or "Follow the Leader".

Before reading a story, determine a clue word (such as the main character's name). The child should raise his or her hand every time the word is mentioned.

SNACKS: French fries or French toast strips, crossed to make "X" shapes

Hot dogs in "X" shapes
Slash a hot dog (**NOT** chicken or turkey) half-way down through the middle. Repeat from the other end, but do not cut the hot dog through. As the hot dog boils, it will curl into an "X" shape.

TRIP: Nature walk

Egg hatchery

Kite flying

LETTER: Y

_____

_____

NUMBER: 12

_____

_____

SCIENCE: Spring weather

Make paper airplanes.

Make paper "helicopters". Cut a strip of paper, 6" by 3". Fold the lower two corners to the center (A). Cut the upper edge down the center about 2" (B). Fold the cut strips in opposite directions (C). Toss the finished helicopter into the air and watch it spin.

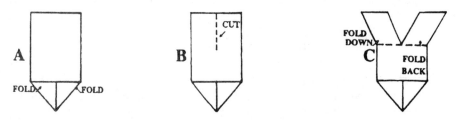

Cut paper into the shapes of different flowers (tulips, daffodils, daisies, roses, etc.). Place these shapes on a piece of art paper, creating an interesting arrangement. Fill a brush with paint and carefully shake the brush over the stencils. When you remove the stencils, the outlines of the flowers will remain in spattered paint.

Make a spring picture. Use cotton balls for clouds or lambs.

Make a rainy spring picture. Draw the picture, then mix water with a bit of blue food coloring. Spatter the colored water on the picture to make rain drops.

Demonstrate rain. (DO NOT LET YOUR CHILD DO THIS ACTIVITY!) Put a pot of water on to boil. While it is heating, put a pie pan into the freezer. As the water boils, put ice cubes in the chilled pan. Hold the pan over the boiling water. The water will condense and drip off.

Make flowers from the separated cups of an egg carton. Cut the edges of the cups to represent the petals of different kinds of flowers. Poke green pipe cleaners through the bottoms of the cups for stems; attach green paper "leaves".

Make a clothespin "butterfly". Cut four 4" squares of colored tissue paper. Decorate a wooden clothespin to represent the body of the butterfly, then gather the squares of tissue paper to fit in the prongs of the clothespin.

Find or draw pictures to represent the different stages of a butterfly's development.

Make a parachute. Tie four pieces of string (about 9" long) to the corners of a handkerchief. Attach the strings to a wooden clothespin or toy character. Roll the handkerchief carefully, then toss the parachute into the air. It should open and drift back down.

STORIES: Rey, H. A. Curious George Flies a Kite.
Seuss, Dr. Yertle the Turtle.

BIBLE STORY: Feeding of the 5000

CHARACTER QUALITY: Generosity

Let your child help plan and execute a project for charity.

SNACKS: Yogurt, for Y

Bread "clouds"
Cut bread into cloud shapes. Spread with cream cheese.

TRIP: Farm (to see newborn animals)

Cloud watching

LETTER: Z

_____

_____

NUMBER: 13

_____

_____

SOCIAL STUDIES: Communities

Make a community, using small boxes for buildings. Discuss types of buildings and the people who work in them.

Write an experience story about your community or about a particular community helper.

Cut pictures of different community helpers from magazines or coloring books. (For an additional challenge, classify these pictures as indoor or outdoor helpers.)

Play policeman as your child rides a tricycle or Big Wheel.

Make a family post office. Let your child make mailboxes for each family member and deliver the regular mail (or notes and pictures sent within the family).

Make a firefighter's hat. Cut a long oval from a piece of red paper (about 20" long and 10" wide). About ⅓ of the way down the oval, cut a semi-circular flap the width of your child's head. Fold the flap up and put the hat on your child's head.

_____

_____

STORIES: Collier, James Lincoln. <u>A Visit to the Firehouse.</u>
Compton, Grant. The <u>What Does a _____ Do?</u> series on community helpers
Lenski, Lois. <u>Policeman Small.</u>
McGinley, Phyllis. <u>All Around the Town.</u>

BIBLE STORY: Jesus and the Children
Zacchaeus, or other character beginning with Z

CHARACTER QUALITY: Joyfulness

Let your child express joy through music. Make up a song! Accompany yourself with rhythm instruments!

SNACKS: Zwieback

Zucchini patties
    Grate 3 zucchini. Add 1 egg, ½ c. fine bread crumbs, ¼ t. salt, and ⅛ t. pepper. Shape into patties. Fry lightly in oil on both sides.

TRIP: Police or fire station

Post office

WEEKLY PLANNING SHEET 28

LETTERS: Review (See pp. 25-27 for ideas.)

_____

_____

NUMBER: 14

_____

_____

COLOR: Blue

_____

_____

HEALTH: Emotions- happiness

The next six weeks will cover common human emotions. _The purpose is for your child to be able to identify and express what he or she is feeling._ _The following activities can be used to teach about emotions, but you should take advantage of everyday situations to encourage your child to talk about his or her emotions._

Draw a picture of (or find in a magazine) a face expressing the emotion, a situation where that emotion might be felt, or an abstract representation of that emotion.

Make a paper-plate face or mask reflecting the emotion.

Identify situations where the emotion might be felt.

Play "Guess My Feeling". Tell a situation and let the child guess what emotion might be felt.

Tell how to help someone who is feeling a negative emotion. If possible or appropriate, follow through with the suggestion (ex., making a card for someone in the hospital).

_____

_____

SOCIAL STUDIES: Community

Play "Charades" to identify different community helpers.

Find or draw pictures of items that would be used by the different community helpers (ex., a hose for a fireman, or a whistle for a policeman). Let your child tell which helper(s) would use a particular item. (This could be made into a game by matching pictures of the helpers with the items you use.) (VARIATIONS: Match helpers with the vehicles they would drive or the hats they would wear.)

Make a simple map of your community, using geometric shapes. (For example, houses might be squares, churches might be triangles, office buildings rectangles, etc.)

Play "Ten Questions". One player thinks of a community helper, and the other asks questions, trying to guess the identity of the helper. Only ten questions may be asked, and they can only be questions that can be answered "Yes" or "No" (ex., "Does he drive a fire engine?").

STORIES: Rey, H. A. <u>Curious George Goes to the Hospital.</u>
Rockwell, Harlow. <u>My Dentist.</u>
Scarry, Richard. <u>Postman Pig and His Busy Neighbors.</u>
Seuss, Dr. (Any book)

BIBLE STORY: The Good Samaritan

CHARACTER QUALITY: Empathy

Tell or read a story where someone is expressing a negative emotion. Ask your child how that person feels.

SNACKS: Soft pretzels, shaped into letters (See Week 5.)

TRIP: Construction site

Parent's workplace

LETTERS: Continue review.

_____

_____

COLOR: Green

_____

_____

SOCIAL STUDIES: Easter

Dye eggs.

Make a "stained glass" cross. Cut two pieces of waxed paper, about 8" long. Let your child **CAREFULLY** use the blade of a blunt pair of scissors to shave old crayons, letting the shavings fall on one piece of waxed paper. When the child has finished, place the other piece of waxed paper on top. An adult should place several layers of newspaper under and on top of the waxed paper "sandwich", then press gently with a warm iron. The crayon will melt, giving the impression of stained glass. Let your child cut the finished waxed paper into a cross shape.

Draw a picture of the first Easter.

Write an experience story about the way your family celebrates Easter.

_____

_____

SCIENCE: Plants

Plant a flower seed in a styrofoam cup and observe it over the next few days. For the more advanced child, you may want to experiment by planting several seeds and placing them in different conditions (dark, cold, dry, etc.). Compare the different plants as they grow.

Color a glass of water with some food coloring. Place the cut end of a celery stalk in the water. Observe the celery draw the colored water up the stalk.

Using pictures or real fruits, let your child match fruits and their seeds.

Put seeds on damp paper towels and seal in Ziploc bags. Tape the bags to a sunny window. Observe the roots and stems as they emerge.

Let your child sort different seeds. Observe similarities and differences.

Compare the leaves of different plants (real or pictured).

Find out which seeds are edible. Try some!

Make a collage, using different seeds, leaves, or flowers.

HEALTH: Emotions- excitement *(See Week 28.)*

STORIES: Easter stories
            Silverstein, Shel. The Giving Tree.
            Udry, Janice May. A Tree Is Nice.

BIBLE STORY: Zacchaeus

CHARACTER QUALITY: Honesty

Act out situations where honesty is required.

SNACKS: Green foods

            Fruits- be sure to examine the seeds!

            Bean sprouts

TRIP: Florist

            Greenhouse or nursery

            Arboretum

            Nature walk to observe plants

NUMBER: 15

_____

_____

COLOR: Purple

_____

_____

SCIENCE: Growth

Gather or draw pictures showing different stages of the life cycle (both human and animal). Let your child mix up the pictures and put them in order.

Gather or draw pictures showing adult and baby animals. Let your child match each adult with its baby.

Make "My Life Story" book. Help your child write the story of his or her own life. Let your child illustrate it, or find old snapshots to put into the book.

Go through your child's baby book or family photo album. Observe how your child (and other family members) have grown and changed.

Begin charting your child's height and weight. Continue measuring every month.

_____

_____

HEALTH: Emotions- jealousy _(See Week 28.)_

_____

_____

STORIES: Johnson, Crockett. <u>Harold and the Purple Crayon.</u>
                McNaught, Harry. <u>Baby Animals.</u>
                Minarik, Else Holmelund. <u>Little Bear.</u>
                Stevens, Carla. <u>The Birth of Sunset's Kittens.</u>

_____

BIBLE STORY: Entry Into Jerusalem

_____

CHARACTER QUALITY: Discernment

Discuss stranger safety. Act out relevant situations.

Act out situations where others ask your child to do something. Help your child determine which requests are right and which are wrong.

_____

_____

SNACKS: Purple foods

_____

TRIP: Hospital nursery

Pet shop

Animal shelter

A family member or friend (perhaps someone your child has not seen in a
       long time)

_____

NUMBER: 16

SCIENCE: Body parts

Have your child watch his body parts move in a mirror (preferably full-length).

Cut out a full picture of a person from a newspaper or magazine and identify the different body parts.

Make your child's silhouette. Tape a large piece of white paper to the wall and seat your child in front of it. Using a strong flashlight or lamp (with shade removed), cast the shadow of your child's profile on the white paper. Trace around the profile with pencil. Cut out the profile and glue to black paper.

Play "Where Is Thumbkin?"

SCIENCE: Musical instruments

Try to find pictures of musical instruments in books and magazines. Discuss how the sounds are made. Help your child learn the names of the most common instruments.

Try to get a recording of different musical instruments from the library. See if your child can identify the instruments from their sounds.

Experiment with different household objects to see which produce musical sounds.

Make a "water xylophone". Fill glasses with varying amounts of water. Tap them lightly to hear the different tones.

Make a simple musical instrument.

SANDBLOCKS- Staple sandpaper onto blocks of wood; rub together

TAMBOURINE- Put dried beans or rice between two styrofoam plates. Staple the plates together along the rims.

DRUM- Decorate an empty oatmeal box or coffee can.

MARACAS- Put dried beans or rice in a Dixie cup. Invert a second Dixie cup over the first and tape together. Push a wooden stick through the top cup and tape securely.

CHIMES- Tie canning rings to a coat hanger. Tap the rings with a pencil or stick.

Blow across the rim of an empty soda bottle. Practice until you can hear a musical tone. Put varying amounts of water in the bottle to see the effect on the tone.

HEALTH: Emotions- sadness *(See Week 28.)*

STORIES: Aliki. <u>My Hands.</u>
               Brenner, Barbara. <u>Bodies.</u>
               McCloskey, Robert. <u>Lentil.</u>
               Prokofiev, Serge. <u>Peter and the Wolf.</u>

BIBLE STORY: Last Supper

CHARACTER QUALITY: Dependability

Give your child a simple task or command. Give praise for being dependable.

SNACKS: Gingerbread boys (Discuss body parts.)

            Thumbprint cookies
               Beat together ½ c. butter, ¼ c. packed brown sugar, 1 egg yolk, and ½ t. vanilla. Stir in 1 c. flour. Cover and chill until firm to handle. Using 1 T. for each, shape dough into balls. Gently press thumb into the center of each ball and fill with about ½ t. preserves (any flavor). Bake at 350° F. until lightly browned (12-15 min.).

TRIP: Music store

            Concert or opera

SCIENCE: Body parts

Draw circles on a piece of paper. Let your child draw in funny faces (OR cut facial features from magazines and glue them in place.)

Have your child make a person out of clay (or bent aluminum foil). Identify the body parts while they are being created.

Have your child lie down on butcher paper or cardboard. Trace around your child. Let your child fill in the outline with correct details. Cut out the finished project and hang on a wall.

Let your child fingerpaint. (See p. 11 for recipes.) As he paints, use the names of the different parts of the hand and forearm.

Play "Head, Shoulders, Knees, and Toes".

Make a Body Parts book. Label each page with the name of a particular body part. Have your child cut pictures of those parts from magazines and glue them on the correct page.

Help your child identify the private (or "no") areas of his or her body.

_____

_____

HEALTH: Emotions- anger *(See Week 28.)*

_____

_____

LANGUAGE: Memorize full name

(During the next few sessions, your child will be learning important information about himself. The best way to encourage memory is through repetition-- FUN repetition! Most of the ideas listed here can also be adapted to the other items of information that you want your child to learn in the next few weeks.)

As you bounce a ball or throw a beanbag to your child, have him repeat his full name.

Give each member of the family 10 pennies (or 10 raisins). Every time a family member asks your child his full name and it is recited correctly, the child is given a penny (or raisin). If he makes an error, he must give up a penny (or raisin).

Sing your child's full name in a made-up tune (or a real one adapted to the situation).

Label (or let your child label) his belongings with his full name. Ask your child to "read" his name every time you pass one of these labels.

Have family members address notes (or pictures) to your child, using his or her full name.

STORIES: Parrish, Peggy. Any <u>Amelia Bedelia</u> book. (She is referred to by full name.)

BIBLE STORY: Crucifixion

CHARACTER QUALITY: Forgiveness

Act out situations where the child could practice forgiveness.

Discuss how forgiveness can restore friendships.

SNACKS: Name writing
            Use tube frosting to write your child's full name on several cookies or a cake. (VARIATION: Use canned cheese spread on slices of bread, rice cakes, or crackers.)

TRIP: Doctor or dentist

         Hairdresser

NUMBER: 18

_____

_____

COLOR: Black

_____

_____

LANGUAGE: Memorize age (Use ideas from last week.)

_____

_____

LANGUAGE: Nursery rhymes

(GENERAL NOTES: Hopefully, you have already been reading nursery rhymes off and on to your child for the past several years. Nursery rhymes are an important part of our cultural heritage and are often a child's first exposure to poetry. Continue to read them to your child, but during these next three weeks make a special emphasis on the characters and recitation of nursery rhymes from memory. Since there are so many, and you want your child to be relatively familiar with them, you may want to divide your favorites into three groups and emphasize a different group of rhymes each week.)

Recite some favorite nursery rhymes, with you and your child alternating lines.

Substitute the names of family members in some favorite nursery rhymes.

Act out some nursery rhymes.

Practice saying nursery rhymes while bouncing a ball.

Have your child draw a picture for a favorite nursery rhyme. (VARIATION: Let your child make his or her own nursery rhyme book; you write the rhymes and let the child illustrate them.)

Draw or find pictures of different objects that different nursery rhyme characters would use (ex., a pail for Jack and Jill, a plum for Little Jack Horner). Let your child identify the nursery rhyme character that would use that particular object.

Show how a nursery rhyme character would do a particular action (such as Jack jumping over the candlestick, Little Miss Muffet sitting on her tuffet, etc.)

Play "Charades", acting out the different nursery rhymes.

_____

_____

HEALTH: Emotions- fear *(See Week 28.)*

_____

_____

STORIES: Nursery rhyme books
               Hoff, Sid. (Any book)
               McGovern, Ann. Black is Beautiful.

_____

BIBLE STORY: Resurrection

_____

CHARACTER QUALITY: Peacefulness

Act out situations in which your child can practice being a peacemaker.

_____

_____

SNACKS: Cottage cheese ("curds and whey")

           Plums ("Little Jack Horner")

_____

TRIP: Newspaper office

_____

WEEKLY PLANNING SHEET 34

NUMBER: 19

_____

_____

LANGUAGE: Nursery rhymes (Choose activities from last week.)

_____

_____

LANGUAGE: Memorize address

_____

_____

SCIENCE: "Crawly Things"

Make a "Bug Keeper". Cut windows in the side of a salt box and cover with pieces of nylon net. Your child may keep insects in the box to observe for short periods of time. *(NOTE: You may also use plastic peanut butter jars with holes punched in the lids.)*

Make a caterpillar from 3 or 4 sections of an egg carton cut out together. Color the sections and glue on eyes and antennae.

Make an ant farm. Punch holes in the lid of a gallon jar and put an ant hill inside. Place moist cotton balls on top of the soil. Place cheesecloth over the mouth of the jar and screw on the lid. Cover the outside of the jar with dark paper when you are not actually observing the ants. Every few days, add some food crumbs to the jar. Keep the cotton balls moist.

Catch a spider's web. Carefully hold a piece of dark paper behind the spider's web and move the paper toward the web until it sticks to the paper. (You may want to spray the web first with white spray paint to make it more visible on the paper.) Spray with hair spray or other fixative.

Fingerplay: "The Eensy, Weensy Spider."

Play "Guess Which Bug". Give clues about an insect and see if your child can guess it.

Sing bug songs, such as "There Was An Old Lady" or "Bringing Home a Baby Bumblebee".

Make a footprint butterfly. Have your child stand on a piece of paper, feet close together. Trace around both feet. Let your child color the footprints to resemble the wings of a butterfly, adding a body and antennae.

104

Discuss the three parts of an insect's body (head, thorax, and abdomen). Cut out the pieces from heavy paper or cardboard and let your child put the insect together.

Make an insect book. Collect or draw pictures of different insects and have your child glue them onto separate pages. Let your child dictate a few sentences about each insect for you to write on the page. (Remember-- a spider is an arachnid, not an insect.)

Be a butterfly! Pin one yard of colorful fabric to your child's cuffs and collar. Make paper or pipe cleaner antennae, and your child can pretend he is a butterfly.

STORIES: Carle, Eric. The Very Hungry Caterpillar.
             Pettigrew, Shirley. There Was An Old Lady.

BIBLE STORY: Paul's Conversion

CHARACTER QUALITY: Inquisitiveness

Take apart an old clock or small appliance.

Introduce your child to the reference section of the library.

Research a topic of interest to your child.

Play "Hide and Seek".

SNACKS: Anything made with honey (for bees)

            Use cherry tomato halves to make ladybugs or caterpillars.

            "Bugs on a Branch" (also called "Frogs on a Log")
                Fill a stalk of celery with peanut butter. Dot with raisins.

TRIP: Beekeeper

          Nature walk to observe insects

WEEKLY PLANNING SHEET 35

COLOR: Brown

_____

_____

NUMBER: 20

_____

_____

LANGUAGE: Nursery rhymes

_____

_____

SCIENCE: Farm animals

Sing "Old MacDonald Had a Farm".

Make a beanbag animal. Cut a simple animal shape from a folded piece of fabric, creating two pieces. Let your child sew or glue the edges. When almost completely closed, add large dried beans, then close the beanbag.

Find or draw pictures of farm animals. Make a farm animal book, or make a mobile by tying strings to the pictures and then to a coat hanger.

Play "Who Am I?" Give clues about a particular farm animal and see if your child can guess the animal.

Play "Charades", acting out farm animals.

See if your child can identify farm animals by their sounds.

Write an experience story about farm animals.

_____

_____

LANGUAGE: Memorize telephone number

Let your child practice dialing your home on a toy telephone.

Write your telephone number on a piece of heavy cardboard. Cover the numbers with glue, then sprinkle on salt. When the glue is dry, let your child run his fingers over the numbers while reciting your telephone number.

Make up a song to learn your telephone number. ("Twinkle, Twinkle, Little Star" and "Old MacDonald" are particularly adaptable.)

STORIES: Any nursery rhyme book
Flack, Marjorie. The Story About Ping.
Gag, Wanda. Millions of Cats.
Lenski, Lois. The Little Farm.
McCloskey, Robert. Make Way for Ducklings.
Potter, Beatrix. (Any story)
Provensen, Alice and Martin. The Seasons at Maple Hill Farm.

BIBLE STORY: Paul's Shipwreck

CHARACTER QUALITY: Discretion

Identify topics that are appropriate only for family discussion (such as family problems, personal information, whether or not parents are home, etc.).

SNACKS: Brown foods

Farm animals
Use farm animal cookie cutters to cut cookies, lunch meat or cheese, or gelatin. (Mix 4 envelopes unflavored gelatin and 3 packages flavored gelatin in a large bowl. Add 4 cups boiling water and stir until dissolved. Pour into a 9 X 13 pan and chill until firm.)

TRIP: Pet shop

Farm

NUMBERS: Review (See pp. 29-32.)

_____

_____

SCIENCE: Zoo animals

(NOTE: Many of the activities for farm animals can be adapted to zoo animals as well.)

Recite "Five Little Monkeys".

Play "I Went to the Zoo and I Saw a _____ ". Take turns reciting the sentence, filling in the blank with the name of a different zoo animal. See how many different animals you can name.

Play "Zoo or Farm?" Have your child separate animal crackers or pictures into the two groups.

_____

_____

SCIENCE: Summer

Draw with colored chalk on the sidewalk.

Make paper fans.

Observe the shadows made by a certain object throughout the day.

Draw or cut pictures to make a collage of summer activities.

Fingerpaint with your feet!

Have your child draw an underwater scene. Cover the picture lightly with blue water color.

Draw or find pictures of equipment needed for different summer sports.

Measure temperature in the sun and in the shade. Compare.

Set up a lemonade or Koolaid stand.

Play "Land or Sea?" Draw or find pictures of different animals. Have your child divide them into the two groups, depending on where the animals live.

Make sunglasses. Cut two of the plastic rings that hold soda cans together. Glue or tape colored cellophane over the rings. Punch holes in the sides and attach pipe cleaners to hold the glasses in place. (For safety, bend in the ends of the pipe cleaners that go over the ears.)

Glue a spool to the center of a paper plate to make a sundial.

If possible, gather and examine different kinds of sea shells.

Place a variety of objects in water to see which will sink and which will float. (You can make a simple chart to help your child learn how to organize information.)

Examine different shadows outdoors. Try to guess which object is making the shadow.

STORIES: Lenski, Lois. On a Summer Day.
McCloskey, Robert. The Little Island.
Rojankovsky, Feodor. Animals in the Zoo.
Seuss, Dr. One Fish, Two Fish, Red Fish, Blue Fish.
Zion, Gene. Harry By the Sea.

BIBLE STORY: Philippian Jailer

CHARACTER QUALITY: Cooperation

Place a large box on the floor. Have your child stand on the opposite side of the box and push at the same time as you do. Now have your child join you on your side and push the box together. Did the box move more easily when you pushed against each other, or together?

When it is time to clean up toys, take toys out of the box as your child is putting them in. Point out how much better it is if you cooperate in putting the toys away.

SNACK: Repeat one of your favorites!

TRIP: Baseball game or track meet

Beach

Camping trip or picnic

Zoo

Fish farm or aquarium

BIBLIOGRAPHY

Anselmo, Sandra; Pamela Rollins; and Rita Schuckman. R is for Rainbow. Reading, Mass.: Addison-Wesley, 1986.

Arnold, Lois B. Preparing Young Children for Science. New York: Schocken Books, 1980.

Bredekamp, Sue; and Carol Copple, eds. Developmentally Appropriate Practice in Early Childhood Programs. Washington, DC: National Association for the Education of Young Children, 1997.

Brenner, Barbara. The Preschool Handbook: Making the Most of Your Child's Education. New York: Pantheon Books, 1990.

Dowell, Ruth I. Move Over, Mother Goose! Finger Plays, Action Verses, and Funny Rhymes. Mt. Ranier, MD: Gryphon House, 1987.

Elkind, David. Miseducation: Preschoolers at Risk. New York: Alfred A. Knopf, 1987.

Galinsky, Ellen; and July David. The Preschool Years. New York: Times Books, 1988.

Muncy, Patricia Tyler. Complete Book of Illustrated K-3 Alphabet Games and Activities. W. Nyack, NJ: Center for Applied Research in Education, 1980.

Rimm, Sylvia. Raising Preschoolers. New York, Three Rivers Press, 1997.

Rogers, Fred; and Barry Head. Mr. Rogers' Playbook. New York: Berkley Books, 1986.

Ward, Ann. Learning at Home: Preschool and Kindergarten. Gresham, OR: Christian Life Workshops, 1987.

Zaslavsky, Claudia. Preparing Young Children for Math. New York: Schocken Books, 1979.

The concept of learning centers may be new to parents, but they can have great value in the home setting. Simply speaking, a learning center is an activity that is designed to be used by the child, independently and without help. It can be used to present a new concept or to reinforce what has been previously learned. Learning centers do take some time and effort to make, but once they are completed they can really enhance your child's educational program.

Packaging Learning Centers

Save the following for storage of your learning centers.

> Egg cartons
>
> File folders
>
> Pringles cans
>
> Large mailing envelopes
>
> Large Ziploc bags
>
> Small gift, card, or hosiery boxes

Kinds of Learning Centers

The kind of learning center you make will depend on the concept you want to present. Consider the following types.

ERASABLE MARKER

You will need to purchase clear Contact paper and erasable crayons or markers. Choose activities where the child needs to write or draw a response (such as tracing his name). You can also use pages from commercially-prepared workbooks or puzzle books. Glue these sheets to heavy cardboard or file folders. Cover them with clear Contact paper and let the child use the markers to do the activity. When finished, you can erase the responses, and the child can repeat the activity again and again. This is especially good for dot-to-dot puzzles, matching activities, practicing letter and number writing, circling groups of objects, etc. Keep these learning centers filed in a large box with the markers.

STRING MATCHING

For these learning centers, you will need yarn or string, and paper brads or Velcro. This type of learning center is for activities that require the child to "draw a line" to match items. Again, you can invent these yourself or use old workbook or puzzle pages. First glue the paper to heavy cardboard, then put paper brads next to the items to be matched (or glue small squares of Velcro next to the items). Tie short pieces of string or yarn to the brads on the left, or stick the string to the Velcro. The child then finds the match on the right and either winds it around the correct brad or sticks the other end of the string to the Velcro square. Like erasable-marker centers, these can also be filed in a large box and used again and again.

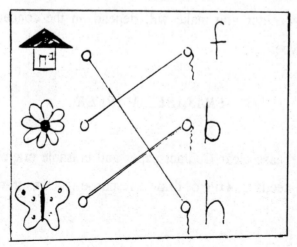

CLOTHESPIN MATCHING

You will need spring-type clothespins for these learning centers. On a piece of heavy cardboard (or around the edge of a paper plate), list one set of items to be matched (ex., capital letters). On the clothespins, write neatly the other set of items to be matched (ex., lower case letters). Let the child clip the matching answer to the cardboard or plate in the appropriate place. These centers can be stored in envelopes, small boxes, Pringles cans, or Ziploc bags.

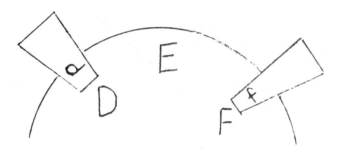

CARD MATCHING

On a strip of cardboard, put a set of items to be matched (ex., picture sets). Make cards for the matching set (ex., numbers). The child can then place the small cards in the correct places next to the large strip. These centers can be stored in small boxes, envelopes, Ziploc bags, or Pringles cans.

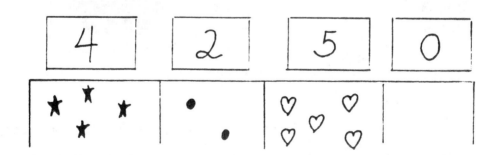

HOOK MATCHING

Inside a small gift box, attach a stick-on cup hook for a set of items to be matched (ex., names of food groups). Put the matching items on small cards and punch holes in the tops of the cards (ex. pictures of different foods). The child can then "hang" the small cards on the correct cup hooks. Replace the lid to the box, and the learning center is ready to store.

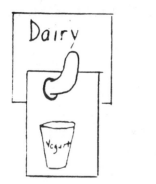  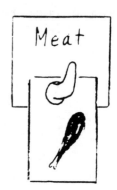

POPSICLE STICK CENTERS

You can make pairs of popsicle sticks to match colors, designs, or textures. Simply mix the sticks up and let your child find the matching pairs. You can also place several sticks together and draw a picture on them, creating a simple jigsaw puzzle. These learning centers store well in Pringles cans, boxes, and Ziploc bags.

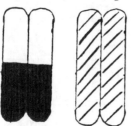 

EGG CARTON CENTERS

Write in the cups of egg cartons and let your child put in small objects or pictures to match. (For example, you could write a number in each cup and let your child count out the correct number of buttons or beans.) Close the lid to make your learning center self-storing.

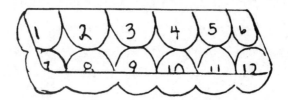

The possibilities for learning centers are endless! More ideas can be found in books such as <u>I Can Do It! I Can Do It!</u>, by LaBritta Gilbert (Mt. Ranier, MD: Gryphon House, Inc., 1984). You might also want to let older siblings make learning centers for your younger children-- fun for the whole family!

APPENDIX B

Tangram

Cut this square into pieces, following the dotted lines. (You may want to glue it to heavy cardboard first.) Use the pieces to make the pictures shown on the next page. You must use **all** the pieces in each picture. As your child works on the pictures, use the names of the shapes as they are placed. If the puzzles prove to be too difficult for your child, simply let him use the pieces to invent pictures of his own.

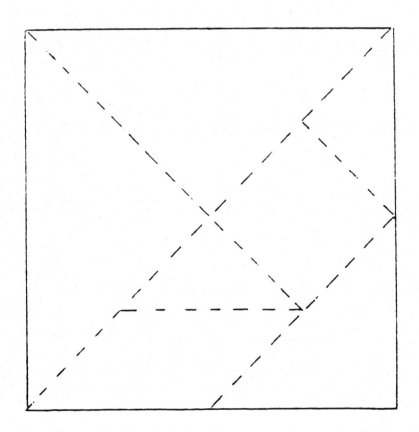

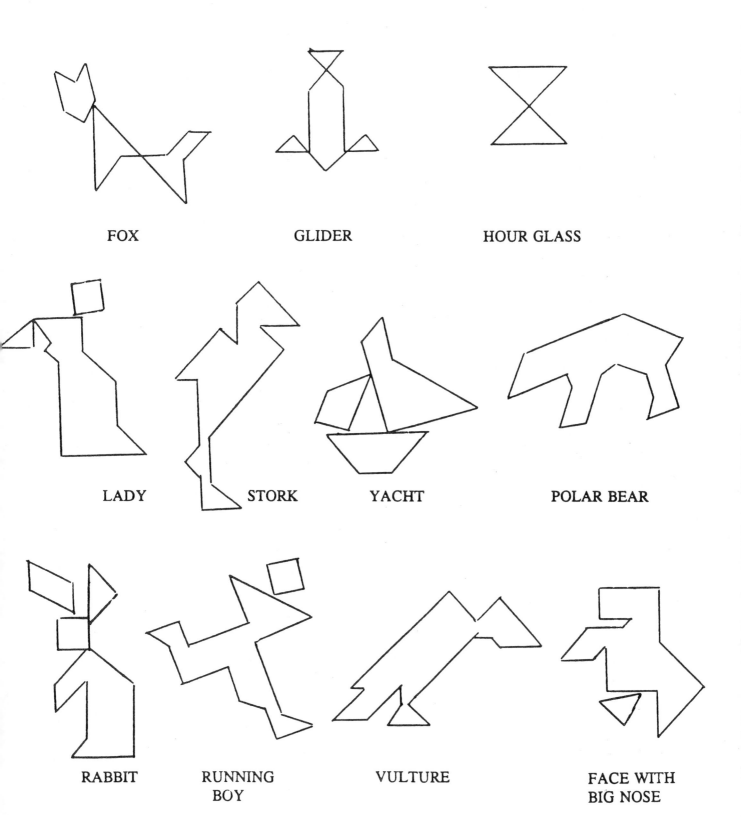

FOX   GLIDER   HOUR GLASS

LADY   STORK   YACHT   POLAR BEAR

RABBIT   RUNNING   VULTURE   FACE WITH
           BOY   BIG NOSE

APPENDIX C

TV and Computers for Young Children

The dilemma of technology is one that is faced by every conscientious parent in our society. While we recognize the educational advantages of technology, we also are aware of its dangers. Is there an appropriate place for television and computers in the lives of preschool children, given what we know about their development?

Television

Television can be beneficial for the preschool child. Programs such as "Mister Rogers' Neighborhood" model positive social behaviors and stimulate the imagination. Worlds of discovery are opened to young minds, stimulating cognitive development. However, it must be remembered that preschool children have difficulty separating reality from fantasy, so care must be taken with the programs they watch. Studies have also shown that watching violence on television promotes aggressive behavior. Furthermore, the time taken to watch television is time **not** spent on reading, play, conversation, or other activities known to be crucial to the development of preschoolers. Overall, a good rule of thumb for preschoolers is that **television time be used in developmentally-appropriate ways**. This means that the time should be limited (no more than three hours per day) and dedicated to programming that will foster their development, not detract from it.

Computers

Additional concerns exist with the use of computers with preschoolers. There is no question that computer usage does improve eye-hand coordination, and the computer can teach many basic skills. Preschoolers especially like to "play with the buttons" on a computer and learn how to "make it work". However, the computer does not allow the kind of "hands-on" learning that preschoolers need, as they cannot actively interact and experiment with the things seen on the screen. In addition, many of the same problems that exist with television also apply to the computer– separation of reality and fantasy, the tendency to imitate aggressive behaviors, passivity, and lost time. Parents who would like to use the computer with their preschooler should again consider using it in developmentally-appropriate ways– over short periods of time (no more than ten minutes at a time) with good programs that are designed specifically for preschoolers. (You can get advice on programs from the people who already using them-- preschool teachers. If you don't know any personally, you could contact a local preschool or college department of education and ask what programs they recommend.) In any event, a parent should **not** go out and buy a computer primarily for the instruction of a preschool-aged child.

Parents with a good understanding of their preschooler's level of development can usually make good decisions about using technology with their children. Television and computer can be used with care to enhance the learning of preschool-aged children.

Additional Programs for Home Instruction

"My preschooler already knows all the letters. What do I do?"

Parents need to be careful with children who are beyond the scope of <u>Early Education at Home</u> because they are probably still not mature enough for curriculum designed for school-aged children. We recommend that parents research and then select a reading program from the list below. The activities from that program can then be substituted for letter activities in <u>Early Education at Home</u>. (NOTE: The lists included in this appendix are not exhaustive, but simply represent selections that this author has found to be developmentally-appropriate for young children.)

Alpha-Phonics
The Elijah Company
1053 Eldridge Loop
Crossville, TN 38558
1-888-2-ELIJAH
www.elijahco.com
(NOTE: Many of the other materials listed in this appendix are also carried by this publisher.)

"Explode the Code" series
Educators Publishing Service
75 Moulton Street
Cambridge, MA 02138
1-800-225-5750
www.epsbooks.com

Learning Language Arts Through Literature (blue book)
Family Learning Center
221 Long Lake Road
Hawthorne, FL 32640
1-800-953-2762

Teach Your Child to Read in 100 Easy Lessons
Simon and Schuster, Inc.
200 Old Tappan Road
Old Tappan, NJ 07675
1-800-223-2348

Similarly, a child may already know his numbers and shapes and have a good sense of pre-math concepts. Parents may wish to get a math curriculum and substitute for the number and shape activities presented in <u>Early Education at Home</u>; note, however, that changes in pacing may need to be made to meet the individual needs of the child. Some programs to consider are listed on the next page.

Math U See (introductory level)
1378 River Road
Drumore, PA 17518
1-888-854-MATH
www.mathusee.com

1-2-3 Math
Home School Resource Center
1425 E. Chocolate Avenue
Hershey, PA 17033
1-800-937-6311
www.hsrc.com

Pre- Math It!
The Elijah Company
1053 Eldridge Loop
Crossville, TN 38558
1-888-2-ELIJAH
www.elijahco.com

Saxon Math (kindergarten level)
2450 John Saxon Blvd.
Norman, OK 73071
1-800-284-7019
www.saxonpub.com

"We want to continue teaching at home. Do you have curricula for older grades?"

There is a wealth of curriculum materials available for home-schooling, with new materials being developed all the time. What's more, these curricula represent a wide range of formats, philosophies, and approaches. For a parent considering home-schooling, the choices can be overwhelming. What we recommend is that parents consult a good book that will walk them through the considerations that need to be made before choosing a home-school curriculum and then present the options that are available. The materials listed below are particularly helpful for those who are new to home-schooling.

Big Book of Home Learning, by Mary
　　Pride
Home Life, Inc.
P. O. Box 1250
Fenton, MO 63026-1850
1-800-346-6322

**Christian Home Educators Curriculum
　　Manual**, by Cathy Duffy
Home Run Enterprises
16172 Huxley Circle
Westminster, CA 92683
714-841-1220

Elijah Company catalog
The Elijah Company
1053 Eldridge Loop
Crossville, TN 38558
1-888-2ELIJAH
www.elijahco.com

Ultimate Guide to Home Schooling, by
　　Debra Bell
Home School Resource Center
1425 E. Chocolate Avenue
Hershey, PA 17033
1-800-937-6311
www.hsrc.com

The sheets on the next two pages may be reproduced for your personal use.

DAILY PLANNING SHEET

Week No. _____ Day _____

Activities: Materials Needed:

_____   _____

_____   _____

_____   _____

_____   _____

_____   _____

_____   _____

_____   _____

_____   _____

WEEK-AT-A-GLANCE

MON.

TUES.

WED.

THURS.

FRI.

INDEX

This curriculum is designed to follow a 36-week school year. However, you may choose to follow a different format, perhaps working year-round, or developing units of study based on your child's interests. You may also be working with older children at home and may want to integrate your younger child's curriculum with theirs. To facilitate alternate plans of instruction, this index lists the different topics presented in the curriculum, indicating in which Weekly Planning Sheet the activities can be found.

I

J

K

L

M

MONDAY, WEDNESDAY	TUESDAY	THURSDAY
9 AM BREAKFAST DRESS QUIET PLAY	9 AM BREAKFAST DRESS QUIET PLAY	BSF
10:15 OPENING*	10:15 OPENING*	11:30 LUNCH
10:30 STORY LANGUAGE SCIENCE	10:30 READING BETWEEN THE LIONS	PLAY
10:45 ACTIVITY— ART	11:00 OUTDOOR PLAY/ GROSS MOTOR	
11:45 MAKE SNACK/COOKING 12:00 / SESAME STREET ↩ 12:30 SNACK/LUNCH ←	12:30 LUNCH	
1:00 PLAY + ZABOOMAFOO	1:00 PLAY	
2:30 NAP	2:30 NAP	2:30 NAP

Opposites	Same/Different	Sorting	Sizes
72 pg 74	pg 46,48		pg 60
1.	1.	1.	1.
2.	2.	2	
3.	3.	3.	
4	4.		2.
5.		4.	
6.		5.	3.
7.			4